THE HOLOCAUST
FORTY YEARS AFTER

Edited by

Marcia Littell
Richard Libowitz
Evelyn Bodek Rosen

THE HOLOCAUST FORTY YEARS AFTER

Edited by

Marcia Littell
Richard Libowitz
Evelyn Bodek Rosen

Symposium Studies
Volume 22

The Edwin Mellen Press
Lewiston/Queenston/Lampeter

Library of Congress Cataloging-in-Publication Data

This volume has been registered with The Library of Congress.

CIP

This is volume 22 in the continuing
Symposium Series
Volume 22 ISBN 0-88946-714-5
SS Series ISBN 0-88946-989-X

A CIP catalog record for this book
is available from the British Library.

Published by The Edwin Mellen Press in cooperation with:

The Anne Frank Institute
P.O. Box 40119
Philadelphia, PA 19106

The Edwin Mellen Press
Box 450
Lewiston, NY
USA 14092

The Edwin Mellen Press
Box 67
Queenston, Ontario
CANADA L0S 1L0

The Edwin Mellen Press, Ltd.
Lampeter, Dyfed, Wales,
UNITED KINGDOM SA48 7DY

Printed in the United States of America

To Franklin H. Littell and Hubert Locke for their pioneering work, making it possible for the world to understand that the Holocaust is a problem which is interfaith, interracial and equally important a problem for their fellow Christians as it is for Jews.

The Editors wish to thank the Macmillan Publishing Company for the inclusion of the poem on page 4 entitled *The Second Coming* (Reprinted with permission of Macmillan Publishing Company from *The Poems of W.B. Yeats: A New Edition*, edited by Richard J. Fiernan. Copyright 1924 by Macmillan Publishing Company, renewed 1952 by Bertha Georgie Yeats).

CONTENTS

FOREWORD

In 1970 a group of Christian and Jewish scholars under the leadership of two Protestant clergymen, Hubert Locke, a professor of Sociology at Wayne State University, and Franklin Littell, Professor of Religion at Temple University, gathered at Wayne State University to share their concerns about topics still largely ignored by the public and the general academic world. Many leaders of Jewish communal organizations felt at that point in time that it was "counterproductive" to engage in the study of such a painful recent event in history. Rather, they felt it was better to put such memories aside, move forward and "bury past history." The study of the Holocaust had an equally limited place within the University, while the German Church Struggle was virtually an unknown subject within the American Christian community.

So significant were the Wayne State discussions that the conference quickly established itself as an annual event. Since that time we have seen a tremendous growth in public interest and concern in all aspects of Holocaust studies. It is doubtful that even the most optimistic of those assembled at Wayne State in 1970 would have predicted the exponential growth of college courses on the Holocaust, the development of curricula for secondary school students, the publishing of learned books and papers, and the widespread observance of Yom HaShoah. With that growth, the Annual Scholars' Conference has continued its unique work, drawing together — from the congregations and the campuses — men and women from the United States, Canada, Israel, West Germany and other countries. Their study is *interfaith*, *international*, and *inter-disciplinary*. Each year, new ground is broken, new questions raised, new responses suggested.

In 1985, the conference brought together over 500 participants in Philadelphia in a gathering which was unique for several reasons. For one, it marked the 15th Annual convening of the Scholars' Conference, an anniversary which ordinarily lends itself to celebration. More significantly, 1985 marked the fortieth anniversary of the end of World War II and the defeat of the Third Reich. It further marked 40 years after the liberation of the death camps, 40 years after the martyrdom of Anne Frank and

Dietrich Bonhoeffer and the multitude of Hitler's last victims, and 40 years after the beginning of a second life for survivors. It was a time for special reflection and evaluation.

The number "40" is of particular significance in Jewish and Christian sacred scriptures. Forty were the days of the flood, Moses' time on Sinai and Jesus' period in the wilderness. Forty years marked the period of David's rule, and Solomon's reign and, before all else, the time of wandering in the desert following the Exodus from Egyptian slavery. "Forty Years" was a generation, the time it took to appreciate the enormity of those events which led from slavery to Sinai to the Promised Land. After forty years, we are finally *beginning* to understand the enormity and complexity of the event known as the *Shoah*, to realize its implications for Jews and Christians alike and to raise the questions which could not be asked until the initial shock had begun to fade and a fearful reluctance to enter the Kingdom of Night had been somewhat overcome.

The essays included within these pages have been selected from the international body of contributors who presented papers at the 15th Annual Scholars' Conference. Space does not permit inclusion of every paper, nor is it possible to duplicate the responses and discussions germinated by three days of presentations. Yet even in their flat form upon the printed page, the challenges are readily apparent. Forty years earlier the killing was finally brought to a halt and the questions began. Today, those questions continue to haunt us.

The initial questions were technical in nature: How could so many people have been killed? What were the processes of transportation, selection, extermination? Who were the individuals in charge? "How" and "What" questions were followed by "Why" queries: Why could God have allowed His People to be slaughtered? Why was the world silent? Even as these questions were raised, others were also challenging us: Why was the Holocaust a matter of significant concern for Christians and not just a "Jewish matter?" Why were the Churches then silent? How could so many Christians have been bystanders?

Perkei Avot warns that while the project be arduous "it is not your task to complete it, neither are you free to ignore it." It is with recognition of this responsibility that the Scholars' Conference continues to gather both individuals and organizations sharing a deep concern that the Holocaust and its assorted issues neither be forgotten nor dismissed to a corner of academic or intellectual ephemera. The Anne Frank Institute of Philadelphia, the North American Section of the International Bonhoeffer Society, the United States Holocaust Memorial Council—as well as representatives of the National Conference of Christians and Jews and Yad Vashem—have all been present at these meetings, sharing in the effort to raise the world's consciousness of the Holocaust and to relate its meaning to other genocides.

The following chapters represent efforts by theologians, historians, legal experts and education specialists. The authors include survivors and members of the generation which has come of age since the camps were thrown open. The public could then no longer feign ignorance of their existence but their message is still being deciphered.

Many of these chapters originated as manuscripts for oral presentation, typescripts were taken from audiotaped transcriptions. At times they were difficult to transcribe. The editors have done their best and accept full responsibility for any resulting errors in transcription.

The editors thank Irene Kohl, Phyllis Sunstein and Drusilla Cohen especially for handling the word-processing.

Special thanks are extended to the following for providing the financial sponsorship required for a conference of such international scope: The City of Philadelphia; Joseph H. Fink, Esq.; The Richard Gingold Foundation; The Harrison Foundation; The Rittenhouse Foundation; The William O. Douglas Institute.

-Marcia Sachs Littell
-Richard Libowitz
-Evelyn Bodek Rosen

INTRODUCTION

Ever since the first Annual Scholars' Conference on the Holocaust and the Church Struggle in 1970, meetings of scholars in that framework have become almost a matter of course. Today, forty years and more after the end of World War II, the subject of the Holocaust is increasingly examined by scholars in different fields and disciplines. Teachers of literature try to deal with the increasing flow of works in prose and poetry in order to interpret them to their students; historians try to probe deeper into background, framework, analogies, causal connections, development and unfolding of events; psychologists and psychoanalysts are entering the field to try and find answers relating to motivations of victimizers, victims, bystanders, and their children and children's children. Films are being produced in increasing number; expression is given to the event in the visual arts, in theater and in music. Many of us are deeply worried about the "popularization" of the Holocaust, which we had tried to advance in previous decades. Does mass information *have* to be vulgarized? Is there no way out?

Whom do scholars reach? In countries such as those of North America, Europe and some others, including Israel, a large and increasing section of the population nowadays acquires a post-high school education. They become the leaders of industry, commerce, the professions, and political life. They will determine the face of human society, if it manages to survive. It would therefore appear to be of some importance to try and influence them, provide them not only with the necessary information—in itself a formidable and daunting task—but with a tool kit of the mind and the heart, that will have in it humanistic values and pre-conditioning of the soul that will stand in direct and conscious contradiction to those evidenced by the Nazi Reich.

Of course, the scholar's ability to do all this is strictly limited—not only by objective conditions, but by subjective ones as well. But it should not be underestimated either. In the Nazi era, intellectuals were the prime link in the transmission belt leading from the Nazi 'true believers' (Christopher Browning's telling phrase) to the masses. Without them the Nazis could not have done what they did. The first major groups to join the Nazi Party were the students and the teachers. So, it is important that we concentrate on these very same groups.

From time to time we are [being] told—'enough!' Who wants to delve into the depths of human depravity on the one hand and suffering on the other hand? Yet, when those who ask us to cease bothering them have had their say, the wave continues to mount. This, as I pointed out already, is not necessarily an unmixed blessing. The *Shoah* is being used and misused by politicians and, yes, by writers, historians, literary critics, and many others. There is no easy way of preventing what is actually sacrilege, the defacing of the memory of those who cannot protest. It is perhaps the task of future meetings to discuss how to define the misuse of the *Shoah* and how to prevent its repetition. Yet this much is clear: the event is of such magnitude that no one can prevent its penetration into the minds of multitudes of human beings, all of whom are affected by it, directly or indirectly, and could be involved in a future event of similar nature, whether as perpetrators, as victims, or as bystanders.

Our problem is how the *Shoah* will be viewed and what lessons will be drawn from it, and that will depend not only on the material we will prepare but chiefly on the questions we will ask. Yaffa Eliach, in her contribution to this volume, talks of the results of an approach to teaching the *Shoah* that was not sufficiently thought out. People, not only children, tend to identify with the aggressor rather than with the victim. Jan Karski, in his contribution, mentions H. G. Wells who, when faced with the information about the destruction of Polish Jewry, asked why it was that 'everybody' hated Jews. Latent antisemitism, unconscious antisemitism, deeply embedded in the culture of Europe and America, has successfully survived Hitler. Aggressions mount everywhere, also among Jews against non-Jews and other Jews. It is essential to mobilize the countervailing forces, not only to stop the dike from bursting, but to build new dikes and push back the threatening waves.

The Scholars' Conferences owe a great debt of gratitude to their *spiritus mentor*, Franklin H. Littell. The problem that he and many of our other Christian colleagues pose is that of the credibility of the Christian faith after the *Shoah*. One might perhaps enlarge that question to include faith as such—any belief, in God or in man. In this sense, the *Shoah* has become a symbol, because it was the most extreme case known to date of the general malady it epitomizes. It is therefore both as content and as symbol of other contents that we must approach it, and Franklin Littell points to the method of dialectical thinking as the only intellectual tool that may enable us to grasp that unity of uniqueness and universality that the *Shoah* includes within itself. *Shoah* was a tragedy of a certain group with its own history and values at a certain time; but the Jews stand for others—not for the first time in their long history. There was a direct precedent to *Shoah*: the Armenian massacres at the hand of the Ittihadist regime in the Ottoman Empire. And there are parallels between Jews and Armenians, of course, not only between the two tragedies. The only difference (apart from so many parallels,) between the two cases was that of the motivation of the perpetrators, as I have tried to point out numerous times. For the Nazis, the Jews were not really human, they were a devilish force threatening the whole world; they were a universal problem, not a German one only. For the Young Turks, the Armenians were a hindrance in the attainment of an imperial objective; history and religion fed into a chauvinistic and murderous concept. But apart from that, the parallels are more convincing than any differences. That means that if Jews and Armenians can be victims, so can anyone. There, one has the unity of uniqueness and universality.

The volume presented here is the result of much thinking and a great deal of research. One has to agree with Elie Wiesel's inspiring comments: "we are indeed helpless, and yet, dialectically speaking, we are stronger than before." And behind his beautiful analysis of Job's predicament there is that which he implies and does not utter: there was an argument between God and Satan, and then an argument between God and Job — but why were Job's children the victims of that argument? Why did they have to die for God to make a point? It is indeed the Jewish heritage that leads us back to Job and into the consideration, the moral consideration, of the Holocaust. But, as Elie Wiesel says, it also leads us back to life, and to our great chance in Israel — a chance not only for Jews, but for Gentiles too. Please read the book — there are things in it worth pondering over in this spirit.

Yehuda Bauer
Hebrew University
Jerusalem

Chapter I

HOLOCAUST EDUCATION AFTER '40 YEARS IN THE WILDERNESS'

Franklin H. Littell

We are often asked why we remember. When Hubert Locke and I were getting the Annual Scholars' Conference started in 1970 and quite literally financing it out of our vest pockets, that was already one of the first questions that arose. The popular slogan then was: Forget the dark past! Concentrate on the present problems and future prospects! And when we went to different offices, including Jewish agencies, to ask for a few hundred dollars to cover mimeographing and mailing, we were told: "Forget it! The Holocaust is past and gone. It's counter-productive and abrasive in Christian/Jewish relations to bring the issue up so much later. Bury it!"

But neither Hubert nor I has ever won any medals for lack of stubbornness — what my mother of blessed memory used to call "stick-to-it-iveness," and so we persisted. At the first conference Elie Wiesel, already our inspiring teacher, gave the keynote. It's a special blessing to have him as our keynoter again on this 15th Anniversary occasion. There are others in this room who shared the first four years with us, when all participants did everything at their own expense, before there were agencies and institutions that wrote concern for the lessons of the Holocaust into their Tables of Organization, before there was a public awakening to the massive import of the murderous assault of Hitlerism upon the Jewish people — and also the assault upon such of the baptized (of the *Heidenkirche*) as stayed Christian in the Nazi Empire during the years 1933-45.

The real question is not the superficial one: Why bother after forty years? The real point is this: after every major event in the history of the people, it took 'forty years in the wilderness' for the people to understand what had happened to them and to begin to fit that consciousness into their oral tradition. The Exodus was like that. For '40 years in the wilderness' the people were talking about minor details and complaining about the food and water and Moses and Aaron. And then the Exodus emerged in all of its massive impact: the tale of emancipation from slavery, of the giving of the Way of Life (*Torah*), of the pilgrimage toward the Promised Land. What was once the experience of a small, particular people, became a paradigm — a lesson about life and death — for all the tribes and peoples with eyes to see and ears to hear.

The Holocaust is like that: an event of such mass that 40 years had to be spent in the wilderness before the sheer mass of the event could emerge in the consciousness of the people, before it could begin to speak to the consciences of sensitive persons of other tribes and nations.

Today we are — in terms of public response to the Holocaust and its lessons — in a quite different situation from that when only a few solitary poets and scholars were seeking to find their way. Neither the polite repressors nor the militant deniers could hold back the tide of human historical consciousness. The deniers of facts (so-called "historical revisionists") and repressors of memory (chiefly the misguided religious, both Christian and Jewish) are still there, but they are on the fringes. This year the Federal government, the governors of all 50 states and the mayors of all major cities, will proclaim and participate in the Days of Remembrance. The numbness of the '40 years in the wilderness' is wearing off rapidly, and survivors, and rescuers and liberators are beginning to speak of the unspeakable, to remember what was once set aside to permit breathing space to get on with life. Under the auspices of the U. S. Holocaust Memorial Council — which is also a primary sponsor of this year's Scholars' Conference — there have been held in the last two years an International Conference of Liberators, an International Conference of Rescuers, and several assemblies of Survivors — which will culminate in an American Gathering of several thousand Jewish Holocaust Survivors here in Philadelphia next month. And soon, in a few short years, a magnificent teaching Memorial Museum will arise in Washington, D. C., — a matching partner to the one already found at Yad Vashem (Jerusalem).

The situation has changed in public. Yet the questions continue to arise: Why do we remember? Why do we teach the Holocaust and its lessons? Why do we talk about these Christians like Probst Lichtenberg and Dietrich Bonhoeffer and Father Delp and Martin Niemoeller who did not bend the kneel to Baal? Why do we hope that the President of the United States, when he visits the German Federal Republic in May, will pay a visit to the Dachau death camp that was liberated by American boys in uniform, and not just to Bonn to be lionized? Why do we lift up the stories of Anne Frank and Hanna Senesh and Mordecai Anielewicz, who perished in the days of their youth, and of Elie Wiesel and Tolka and Abba Kovner and Fejgele Peltel, of Franz Hilderbrandt and Eberhard Bethge, who are still with us — those who lifted up candles in the darkness, that are of their generation who are still alive, not to be left in the Stygian darkness of a Manichaean world? Christian or Jew, they showed us that under the most desolate of circumstances there were those who main-tained courage, affirmed life, gave testimony to the eventual defeat of the forces of the Evil One and to the final mending of the world (*Tikkun ha Olam*).

Even though a great teacher of the Way (*Torah*) put it succinctly— "Forgetfulness leads to exile, while remembrance is the secret of redemption." (*Baal Shem Tov*)—we need the affirmations of those martyrs and witnesses in order to re-form and reconstruct our own lives in the shadow of Auschwitz. That reformation and reconstruction is at once deeply personal and individual, and it is also social. We who still dare to be professing Christians have to deal with the fact that these terrible crimes were committed in the heart of Christendom, by baptized Christians—never rebuked, let alone excommunicated. And we who love *alma mater* have to deal with the fact that those who planned, organized and supervised these terrible crimes were not ignorant, illiterate, superstitious savages: they were products of the German universities before the Nazis got their hands on them, while they were still among the best universities in the world.

What are the Christian preachers and teachers doing to reform and reconstruct their work and their message? What are the universities doing—especially perhaps the American universities—to indicate that they are not content merely to turn out millions of alumni who are technically competent barbarians, immune to the pangs of conscience, the claims of religion, the disciplines of professional ethics?

We need the message of the survivors, of those who have built a second life, to help us affirm life. We need the stories of the heroes and martyrs, to give us eternal reminders that there were those who were surrounded by darkness far more intense than most of us can comprehend— and still affirmed the dignity and integrity and liberty of the human person. We need the reassurance that others, in more difficult circumstances than ours, have faced moral confusions and ethical distortions like those today—and have swum against the current, not floated with the current like dead fish, belly-up.

We need to remember those who affirmed life, and to honor the survivors who built a second life, because we live in a life-denying century. The engines of death dominate our tax structures and make our instrument of government lopsided. Wars and rumors of wars dominate the public media. Hal Lindsey's *Late, Great Planet Earth* has sold over 18,000,000 copies and is still running as a best seller. And many of the figures who typify the age display that reversal of values that was so complete in the Kingdom of Night: the teacher who betrays the youth, the policeman who brings violence rather than order, the doctor who kills rather than heals, the clergyman who waffles the truth, the disloyal general, the politician who never emerges from behind the mask unless he is caught out.

At the turn of the century, W. B. Yeats caught the emerging mood of this century of world war, dictatorships and genocides:

Turning and turning in the widening gyre
The falcon cannot hear the falconer;
Things fall apart; the centre cannot hold;
Mere anarchy is loosed upon the world,
The blood-dimmed tide is loosed, and everywhere
The ceremony of innocence is drowned;
The best lack all conviction, while the worst
Are full of passionate intensity.

Surely some revelation is at hand;
Surely the Second Coming is at hand.
The Second Coming! Hardly are those words out
When a vast image out of *Spiritus Mundi*
Troubles my sight: somewhere in the sands of the desert
A shape with lion body and the head of a man,
A gaze blank and pitiless as the sun,
Is moving its slow thighs, while all about it
Reel shadows of the indignant desert birds.
The darkness drops again; but now I know
That twenty centuries of stony sleep
Were vexed to nightmare by a rocking cradle,
And what rough beast, its hour come round at last,
Slouches toward Bethlehem to be born?

What life-destroying creature, what life-denying engine, is today awaiting its appointed hour?

Eugen Rosenstock and Franz Rosenzweig were the participants in a famous friendship. Rosenzweig was the author of *Star of Redemption*, teacher of Martin Buber, leader of the Frankfurt *Lehrhaus*, ardent student of the Scriptures. Rosenstock was author of several important books of political philosophy, teacher for many years at Dartmouth. The correspondence of their younger years in Germany, which dealt decades ago with many of the issues considered vital today in the Christian/Jewish dialogue, has been published.

Rosenstock later related the second turning point in his life, telling of how he came to America. He was still in his homeland and was visited by a friend of his student years who was wearing the SS uniform. They discussed the economic crisis of the Depression, the difficult political situation, the collapse of public and private morality, the decline of parliamentary democracy into sectarian strife. "Yes, yes," said the SS man. "I agree with you on all of these things. But there is one thing you must realize: Hitler is *the Christ*." There was the blasphemy that led to genocide. There was the idolatry that the men of Barmen courageously condemned.

And Eugen Rosenstock later spoke of this apocalyptic instance to friends, the second turning point in his own life as clear to him as by a special revelation: "In that moment I knew I must leave Germany."

What rough beast, spiritual successor to the terrorist movement that became a criminal government in the Third Reich, is today waiting to be born? And where...? Surely one of the most important lessons of the Holocaust is the necessity of developing an *Early Warning System* on potentially genocide movements, and of dealing with them early enough, while they can still be rendered impotent with a minimum of ripping and tearing in the social fabric.

Fifteen years ago we called for a cooperative effort that should unite educated persons of conscience: interdisciplinary, interfaith, and international. And we pointed especially at the imperative need for a reconstruction of religious philosophy and action, and a reconstruction of the modern university. The foundation remains the same. The challenges remain the same. What has changed is that we are no longer a handful of concerned scholars: we have become a multitude. And now we are confronted by a second task: to hew to the main goals and profound purpose that first brought us together, to keep the story and the lessons of those years from being vulgarized, cheapened, misused and exploited for base purposes.

Finally, on this side of the watershed — once the massive range has been traversed and we perceive ourselves to be this side of the Holocaust years — we are concerned for the formation of a new and more sensitive human person. We have seen the consequences of the *Eiskalt* technocrat that Himmler praised, the arrogantly curious scientist (Adrian Leverkuhn) that Thomas Mann lined out in *Doktor Faustus*. We want our children and grandchildren to know better years of human interaction than we have seen in our own season. We want to see justice roll forth as waters and righteousness as a mighty stream, and harmony (*Shalom*) triumph over violence and wickedness, exploitation and machine-like indifference to the integrity and dignity and liberty of the human person.

What is required of the person who would stand upright in seasons of great wickedness? Is some secret wisdom required? What do we hear when we listen to the voices that emerge from the records of the Holocaust years? Joep Westerweel was a Dutch Christian (Plymouth Brethren) and a martyr. In his last letter from prison he wrote:

> Anybody who takes part in the persecution of the Jews, whether voluntarily or against his will, is looking for an excuse for himself. Some cannot give up a business deal, others are doing it for the sake of their families; and the Jewish professors must disappear without protest, for the sake of the university....
> I have to go through these difficult days without breaking,

but in the end my fate will be decided and I shall go like a man.

When Dr. Ringelblum, Warsaw ghetto historian and Jewish martyr, spoke to himself and his friends in exhortation (which he seldom did), this is how he phrased the message: "Let it be said that though we have been sentenced to death and know it, we have not lost our human features." Two years ago the City of Berlin honored an elderly lady who had saved Jews. When the newspapermen asked her why she had done it, she replied simply, "Out of self-respect." All of these testimonies, and many others, add up to a simple insight: the vital component is gathered up in the great word, *Menschlichkeit*.

There have been those, across the years, who have insisted that in our Scholars' Conferences we must be rigidly "objective" and "scientific," that we should avoid anything that smacks of involvement (*engagement*) in the social and political struggles of the day. Let me say without embarrassment that for me the personal dimension of this association, yes, I will say "fellowship," has been as important as the intellectual. I know of no more blessed company than those who are inspired but unassuming in the pursuit of Truth, who are able to practice mutual aid in the effort to move us all—and humankind itself—out of the ditch of defamation, persecution and destruction onto the high road which leads to that City whose builder and maker is God.

Chapter II

SOME WORDS FOR CHILDREN OF SURVIVORS: A MESSAGE TO THE SECOND GENERATION

Elie Wiesel

With your permission, I would like to tell you the story of a man that you know, and of his family that you don't. The name of the man is Job, and the name of the family—well, let's wait for his family. I am convinced that all of you have studies the book, and all of you have been disturbed by all the questions—philosophical, metaphysical, theological—that the book implies. However, few of us realize that the real tragedy of Job begins *after* the tragedy. At one point we are told that Job suffered; we are told how he suffered. He lost his belongings, his health, his children, and he and his wife remained alone, for no reason whatsoever. Then, his friends came to see him and only then did his agony begin, when he realized that he had no family. Afterwards he spoke to God, he gave in to God, and we are told in the Book of Job very naively that, at the end, God decided to compensate him for all the pain inflicted upon him, and once again he had children, seven sons and three daughters, and once again he became a happy man.

I don't believe it.

I do not believe that Job became a happy man. And if I were to write a sequel to the Book of Job, Volume Two, I would begin at the place where the story ends. What happened to his children? I mean to his *second* children? How could they live in a house filled with tragedy? How could Job and his wife live with their memories? Why is the story so short? Why did the story give us a happy ending which we cannot believe? Therefore, the real tragedy which follows the other tragedy is the tragedy of Job's children, the children of the survivors.

At this point we are entering into very much the subject I am supposed to deal with tonight: to give a message to children of survivors. Before doing so I would like to open the parentheses. I would like to admit to the mind events that occurred not 40 years ago, but 15 years ago, when Franklin Littell and Hubert Locke decided to have an annual meeting of scholars to explore the theological and religious implications, applications and dimensions of the greatest tragedy that ever occurred in recorded history. I attended that meeting. Why? Because there was something in Franklin Littell's tone of invitation that prevented me from saying no. In fact, there is something still there because I still can't say no—the proof: I'm here now. I remember that day very well, because we had a strange confrontation with another theologian who tried to convince everybody that God is dead. And somehow I was not convinced. So that seminar turned into a confrontation between two views of God. Later that evening I was supposed to go back to New York and the co-chairman of that evening, Hubert Locke, drove me to the airport, a trip that usually takes 35 minutes took 12. And if I'm still here, I have to say a prayer of gratitude. Whenever I think of him, I think of you, all of you, with gratitude.

What else? It's forty years, and forty years, as you know, is a special date in the Bible. Forty years in the Bible is one generation. That means that we are now duty bound to take stock, look back and see what happened in forty years, what happened to us, what happened to the world...what happened to our message...what happened to what we tried to communicate...what happened to the memories we tried to share....

Here I must say that my responses, my attitudes, are ambivalent. On one hand, I am pleased—we all are. Forty years ago nobody wanted to hear our story. And therefore we couldn't tell it. Fifteen years ago, only fifteen years ago, nobody wanted to hear your story or mine, and therefore it was so difficult to organize the group, a group so devoted, of committed scholars—I mean committed to humanity, committed to memory, committed to intellectual honesty. And today, today everybody talks about it. Today it has become the most fashionable subject in many programs. It has become popular: on television stations, in films, in novels, in musicals. Should we be pleased? I am not entirely pleased. I am worried: if you open the gates, the gulf will flow, and whatever has been sacred may become profane, whatever should be pure may become impure. Now millions of people may listen, but once they turn the channel, they change the program, and their interest goes elsewhere.

So what are we to do then: succumb to ratings? As a son of the Jewish people, I submit to you that we always choose substance, not numbers. Forgive me for reminding all of us about something, that if we Jews had chosen numbers 2,000 years ago, we would have become Christians. I do not believe that that is what we must do. I believe that we must try to tell the truth. There is a marvelous saying by a very great scholar in Judaism, the Gaon of Vilna: *Tachlit hageulah, hi geulat haemet*, the purpose of redemption is the redemption of truth. That is real redemption, to redeem truth. And that is a redemption that we are capable of accomplishing if we are ready for it. Are we? Can we comprehend truth?

Forty years ago nobody listened. Now many more listen. The question is *what* is everybody listening to? It may sound paradoxical. Forty years ago the world went through an apotheosis of hope. I was very young then, I was in Paris, a young student, without anything, without friends, and without any knowledge. I had literally come from a strange universe straight to Paris. I remember the hope, the climactic hope, which had filled us all, thinking that now the world had at least learned something. At least now the world knows that if you start to hate and to torture at certain points in this world, then the world will lead to Auschwitz; that if you start with hating one group you will end up hating other groups, that if you start killing one people you will end up killing other people. And we were convinced then that never again, never again, would children die of starvation, that never again in our lifetime would people hate one another, and hate become the law of the land, never. We were *convinced* then that a new era, maybe a messianic era, or a pre-messianic era, was dawning upon humankind, and people would be friends to one another, for we had been brothers to one another, of one another, in those times of darkness. If anyone had told us then that in our lifetime you and I would have to fight antisemitism, covert and open antisemitism, nobody would have believed it. If anyone had been told then that in our lifetime we would have to fight racism, nobody would have believed it. If anyone had told us then that once more people would have to fight a war, nobody would have believed it. If anyone had told us then that we would see children dying, my God, dying in front of our eyes on the television screen, and they would go on dying, and not enough would be done to save them, who would have believed that? Now we know that violence has once more become divinity-like, the religion of our century. We have seen what fanaticism is doing. Can you imagine that there are 40 wars in the world today? Do you know that the war with Iraq and Iran has already cost more than one million human beings? As for Nazis, there are armed Nazi groups in our own land, on every continent. In Idaho they are arming, they are grouping, they are computerizing the forces. So what happened to our message? What happened to our lesson? To our testimony?

As I told you, my feelings *are* ambivalent. On one hand, I am glad that we spoke, that we had the strength to speak. On the other, I am rather desperate 40 years later. I do not believe that in 40 years the world has learned history. What the world has learned in 40 years is technology. In science we have made extraordinary progress. We have advanced thousands of years in 40 years, but we have not achieved the same amount of progress — not at *all* — not even a thousandth percent of it — in matters of morality or of memory.

So then what do we do? Should we give up? Had Job given up, the book would have stopped in the beginning. And I am convinced that book would not have stopped in the beginning. And I am convinced the book would not have been included in our canon. But Job did not give up. When Job lost everything — he even lost his debate with God — he had children (with the same wife), and therein I respect Job. For Job had all the reasons in the world already then to say to God, "Master of the universe, thank you. You want me to have children again? No. You can force me to pray to you. I will accept it. But you *cannot* force me to have more children, for I have seen what you have done to them. They did not sin. I may have sinned (and even that is disputed in the Bible — Job had not sinned) — but the children have not. Why did you punish them? Why did you slay them?"

My friends, I belong to a people and to a tradition that invested everything it had in our children. I could quote tales and stories on end, from Scripture and Talmudic stories, showing what we have done with our children and for our children. We have placed them almost at the throne of God. A child is born only when God decides that the child should be born. It is God who keeps what we call the Treasure Chest of Souls. God has the key. It is God or his angel who is the guardian of the child when the child comes down. What then do we say about *Tinokot shel beit Rabbanu*, children who go to school? Redemption may come thanks to those children. When Moses ascended to heaven, asking for the law, the angels tried to oppose him. God gave the law to the people of Israel only when Moses assured Him that the children of Israel will be its guarantors. The children. He placed the entire burden of the law, the future of the law, on the shoulders of those children. In Talmudic times, when the Romans occupied Judea, persecutions occurred day after day; despair reigned from one corner of the land to another. We are given descriptive images of how people dealt with the situation. Whenever a master would go in the street, he would stop a child and say, "What did you study today?" The master didn't need the child to tell him, he knew what he studied, but he needed to hear the voice of the child. It was the child who gave him courage, who gave him strength, confidence, the sense of beauty by simply repeating a sentence. And says the Midrash that the sentences uttered by the child became prophetic. The prophets were the children, and therefore the enemy always knew where to hit us.

We are told in our ancient literature that Pharoah wanted to oppress and kill our people. The first target? The children. Any killer who emerged in Jewish history always sought to destroy the children first. Haman: his first target, again — the children. Nebuchadnezzar: the children. And the latest, Hitler: the children. The first to go, the first to be singled out, were the children, and woe unto us; we have lost one, or one-and-a-half, million of them.

Why? Why the children? Why? I can never forget the marvelous Midrash about Jewish suffering in Egypt. When God decided to shorten exile in Egypt, do you know how He did it and why He did it? At one point, Pharoah decided to capture Jewish children and bury them alive in the pyramids. But we are supposed to have a guardian angel in heaven: Gabriel or Michael. Says the Midrash, with its exquisite imagination, that

Gabriel or Michael caught a Jewish child, already disfigured, in mid-air, and brought him before the select celestial showing him to God. Says the Midrash, at that point God couldn't take it, and although the Jews should have stayed in Egypt 400 years, and this happened after only 210 years, God decided there and then to put an end to the torment, and redeem His people. When I read this story in the text, at first I felt so proud of the angel, and proud of the child and so proud of God. But when I reread it a second time I resisted it. I said to myself, there's something wrong here. Where were the angels when our children were killed? If one child was enough to move God to compassion, what about a million children? They moved no one to compassion. The whole world remained apathetic to the plight and the agony and the death of Jewish children.

I'm sure you have heard enough, you have read enough, and you are going to hear tomorrow from scholars who will speak at your conference about the insensitivity to Jewish victims on the part of friendly governments and people. Our own country could have saved thousand of Jewish children and did not; there were people, good people, who made such suggestions, who made such demands, but it was to no avail. The answer was always no. Only the killer was interested in Jewish children, not friends. Therefore, I cannot tell you what men and women of my generation feel when confronted with Jewish children today. When I see a child I'm so vulnerable that the child can do with me anything that he or she wants, and often they do. I accept. Why? I smile and I cry at the same time. For I see in them, behind them, beyond them, I see someone else always.

Let me give you a story. That story is actually very dramatic for me because it took place a few years ago. I was teaching at City College then, and most of my students at that time happened to be children of survivors. In the beginning I did not know, I didn't know why they registered for my courses. Then I understood. They couldn't speak to their parents, their parents couldn't speak, were afraid of speaking, would be embarrassed....Therefore they came to me, they came to my classes, although I rarely teach Holocaust literature and I admire all of you who do. I cannot tell you how grateful I am to any teacher who teaches the subject, for I cannot. And still the young students came: somehow in their minds I took the place of their father. I became a substitute because I listened to them.

One day a student wished to see me. He was one of my best. He came to my office, closed the door; he looked disturbed; he was pained. He said, "Listen to me, sir. My father was married before the war. His wife and his children died. My mother was married before the war. Her husband and her children perished during the war. They met after the war in a DP camp. They got married, and they had a son — me. But I know that whenever they look at me, it is not me they see." And he cried and cried bitterly.

That explained to me so many mysteries about children today. The children feel that they came in place of other children. Therefore their life is a sorrowed life. They live their own existence but also the existence of their brother, their sister, or a parent or a grandparent. Therefore that's why they are so special. They are more sensitive than their peers. They are more refined than their friends. Their wounds are open, and yet they don't show them. In the course of the years I came to know some of them; I came to love all of them. I've seen so many tragedies that it's almost unbearable to talk about them. One student, a child of survivors, couldn't take it; one morning he took a typewriter, hung it on his throat, and ran into the sea and drowned. Another one jumped from the eighth floor. And a third, and a fourth. They couldn't take it, because to be a survivor is not easy in a world that doesn't want to listen. And to be a child of survivors is equally difficult in a world that doesn't want to remember. All of a sudden children realize that their parents were not strong, but weak, terribly weak. What does it mean for a child to know that his or her father was humiliated by the enemy to the point of eating potato peels? What does it mean to a child to realize that his or her mother was humiliated to the point of being disfigured, not looking human? What does it mean to children to realize that parents, who are suppose to offer a source of strength, or direction, that their parents in times of stress, were lost, totally lost? Abandoned? For these children, for some of them, the tragedy was so great, so deep, and so piercing they gave up on life. Fortunately, they represent a minority, a small minority. Most of the children of survivors grew up normally, grew to become marvelous human beings. After the first crisis, they overcame the pain and the nightmares and integrated society; they are lawyers, teachers, physicians, philanthropists, philosphers, and professors. One of the great miracles of our time is that our children have not become criminals, have not become nihilists, have not become anarchists; and do you know why? — because their parents did not become nihilists, did not become anarchists, did not become criminals. Logically they should have. Logically, when we came out of the war, 40 years ago, and saw civilization in ruins, saw that all the ideals betrayed humankind, that the image of God was the image of cruelty; when we realized that our friends were no friends, that our allies were not concerned with our fate; when we realized that culture meant nothing; that art meant nothing; oh, we realized so many things. But then, why not turn to crime and violence? Why not say we shall take the law in our own hands and we shall act accordingly?

We didn't. Quite the opposite.

Immediately after the war we reintegrated our old society and this, any psychiatrist will tell you, is not normal. For to go through such upheavals — the shock of contradiction, the shock of opposites, from home right away to the camp, from camp right away to liberation — should have produced a generation of mentally unbalanced people. It didn't. Many went to Israel and joined the Haganah and began building, rebuilding, the sovereignty of an ancient people with pride and honor and compassion. Others joined the Communist Party (in Eastern Europe). They didn't know about the murders of the Communist Party; they went to the Communist Party believing they must re-create a world, they must reveal the ideals of Isaiah and Jeremiah in political terms, they must change the world; therefore they joined the Party until they too were arrested and executed by communist leaders. Others came to the United States, France, Australia, New Zealand, and elsewhere. They became leaders in their own society, in their own community. To me, that is a miracle. I would have expected Job after the tragedy to be mentally deranged, and his children too.

So what do we learn from this? We learn some important lessons: that the enemy *was* stronger than we were. We must say that because it's true. One killer with a machine gun has more power than a thousand scholars with words of truth on their lips and philosophy in their minds — one machine gun is stronger...and they used it. But we have also learned that after the conquest, after the tempest, it is up to us to determine the outcome of the struggle. After the struggle, whoever has faced a thousand killers may proclaim his or her victory over them, if he or she remains human.

What else can we learn? We can learn that the laws of normalcy do not apply necessarily to all people in all times. *We* determine what is human.

So there are already some lessons which I think the children of survivors, the next generation, can learn and have learned. There are others. What are they? Simple things, first of all. One, never to turn anything into an abstraction. The German SS professors lost their humanity when they allowed themselves to turn human beings into abstractions. Human beings are not abstractions. And whenever they are being made into abstractions, you may be sure that the experiment will go wrong, either in Russia or in Germany. A human being is unique. Every human being is unique. No human being is replaceable. Every one of us is mortal, but one minute before we die we are immortal.

What else? We must learn the importance of words. My friends, remember that less than 20 years elapsed between Hitler's *Mein Kampf* and the Final Solution. In 20 years the words gained momentum, the abstract words became concrete, and ultimately we were victims not only of people but of their words.

What else did we learn? We learned never to be neutral, never to be silent when other people's lives or dignity are at stake, for neutrality in times of stress and danger never helps the victim, it always helps the executioner. If the world had been less complacent in the '30s, less neutral with regard to evil as it reigned already in Germany, the Final Solution would not have taken place.

And what else have we learned? We have learned that evil must be unmasked right away. We have learned that this is what we teachers must do: we must train our students and we must train their parents to uncover, to unmask evil for the abomination it is; when we unmask it, it must not be given a second chance. We must fight it right away. With all the means that are at our disposal. As educators we must unmask evil educationally; as philosophers, philosophically; as moralists, with our moral weapons; but we must fight. Don't give evil a chance.

What else? We as Jews must also learn not to link our present era of creativity and joy—I mean Israel—to the tragedy in Europe. I could not believe that one is a consequence of the other although I know it is. I don't want to know it. However, it is up to us now to see in Israel the dream of our dreams, the sap of our lives; and therefore, to you children of survivors, Israel must be the sacred fire that keeps you awake at night. In that order, we must proclaim our solidarity with all our brethren and sisters everywhere. The Jews in Russia who suffer—we must help them. The Falashas need help—we must help them. Jews are in jails in Syria— we must help them. In other words, because of the privilege which is yours, you must use that privilege to help Jewish people, our people, everywhere. However, I plead with you, do not make it exclusive. Our concern for our people must be our first priority but not our only priority. We must help all people who suffer, and we must be for all people who are persecuted. If we try to help the Falashas in Ethiopia, it is right, but I *plead* with you to help all the other mothers and children and parents and grandparents who are not Jewish but who die of starvation in Ethiopia. They too must be our priority. And if we help Jews in Russia we must also try to help non-Jewish dissidents who are oppressed. We must help Sakharov who is exiled; he is not Jewish but he needs our help and deserves our help. Priority, yes; exclusivity, no. And this again is the lesson.

My good friends, if you were to decide not to do so, nobody could force you. You have paid your dues, you or your parents have. And if you were to say to the world, "Listen, we don't owe you anything anymore, now we want to live happily. Pursuit of happiness is guaranteed to us as well. We want to live in peace and we want to be concerned only with our children and with our people; let someone else take care of the others because no one took care of us." If you were to say that, no one could blame you. But I plead with you not to use that argument. You must be worthy of the suffering that you inherited, and the suffering that we inherited is such that it must transcend groups, it must transcend communities, and the more Jewish our memory is, the more universal it becomes. I know, I know it's not easy. I know it's not easy for children of survivors to continue, or even to begin. I've seen them. I've seen them so that I've written a novel about them. The novel that Marcie Littell mentioned is about children of survivors, because for years and years I've tried to live their pain and to absorb it. I've seen children who felt so sorry for their fathers that it created an unnatural relationship between fathers and children. At one point the children became the parent of their parents. That is too much to ask of them. And yet we are asking the impossible of them. We are because they have learned. They have learned that what we receive must be shared, what we have gotten must be communicated. And then there is one lesson above all the others: whatever we have seen and endured must never be used against humankind. If we were to use it against humankind, we would betray our suffering. Suffering confers no privileges. Remember that. It's only what you do with it that matters. And you children have proven to me, to us, that you don't abuse it, you don't use it, you are sharing it for the sake of others.

Here I come to one more point to which Franklin Littell alluded earlier at another lecture that he gave, when he spoke about the need to fight trivialization and vulgarization. Thank you, my friend. Fourteen, fifteen years ago, I spoke about it then, already. I don't know why, in 1970, I wrote about it in my book, *One Generation After*. I felt that the trend was toward vulgarization. Why? Because maybe it's easier to accept, it's easier to read, it's easier to absorb, it's easier to understand. Vulgar things are always easier than substantive things. I would suggest to you, children of survivors, that now it must be your duty to fight vulgarization. Don't allow it to prevail. It's too early. Some of us are still alive and we remember. And there is an amount of suffering that by its very magnitude commands respect, and ours is such a suffering. It is for you now to protect that treasure, that heritage, that legacy, which we are giving to you, and we are giving it to you because we have no choice. Oh, believe me, I would so much rather write novels about a boy and girl who fall in love, or about the American adventure, or the Jewish adventure — happy novels, romantic novels. I would so much rather try to make you smile than weep. What can we do? Time is going too fast, and we see it, we see it, literally, physically we see it, we see what is happening to our memory. I think there is a passage in Gabriel Garcia Marquez' *A Hundred Years of Solitude* where he says a whole village has been cursed, and the curse is that they forget. I'm afraid of that curse. I'm afraid of the malediction. I'm afraid of people who forget, and even of those who use that forgetfulness for their ugly purpose. You know as well as I do that those who deny our experience multiply at an astonishing rate. There are hundreds of them, thousands of them all over the world, who do nothing else. They devote their lives to forgetting and making other people forget, just as we devote our lives to remembering and making other people remember. Hundreds of books have appeared in dozen of languages trying to prove that what we have lived through did not take place. I must tell you what I think of them now. What do they think of us, how insensitive could they be to our fate, what do they think that we feel? I could never dignify them with a debate. I don't think that you should. You must fight them, and the only way to fight them is with memories, remembering, and in keeping the memory alive and dignified.

Now, you are not alone. You are not alone and you have allies and friends. And the fact that we met tonight under the auspices of this conference proves to you that you have friends. And you know how grateful we are to those friends. We Jews are a people imbued with a sense of gratitude. No other people is as capable of gratitude as we are. And we are grateful to these friends, because they are a minority in their own milieu, in their own entourage, in their own community, just as we Jews are a minority in the large community of nations. Hence the bond of friendship and gratitude between us.

In conclusion, my good friends, I must confess something which may surprise you. I must confess my helplessness. I have written 25 books, the latest one is the 25th, and I must tell you that all the questions that I asked in my first are open, and valid, even now. Not one question has been answered. Not one doubt has been dispelled. All that I wanted to know then I still want to know now. What I didn't understand then I don't understand now. I still don't understand how a people could become overnight a people of accomplices of killers. I still don't understand how so many friendly nations remained insensitive to the murder of a people. I still don't understand why the Allies did not bomb the railway stations. I still don't understand why the Russian people didn't bomb the railway lines. They were closer to Auschwitz than the Americans were. That does not exonerate either, but the question becomes more important. I still don't understand how we survived. I still don't understand why so many of us yielded, and how so many of us did not.

In speaking of children, I am reminded of a great poet called Itzhak Katznelson, the one who wrote "The Song of the Slaughtered Jewish People," one of the great elegies of the period. He wrote that one day a monument should be erected to the memory of the Jewish child smuggler. Do you know that those children, eight, nine, ten years old, saved the Ghetto from hunger and starvation because of their smuggling? They were so small, they could sneak out through the holes in the Ghetto walls. And do you know what the killers would do? We have it from Curzio Malaparte who witnessed the occupation. He speaks about them in his book, *Kaputt*. After their dinners, after their festive dinners, SS killers would go to the Ghetto walls and hunt those children. They would go on hunting expeditions after their dinners, shooting those little children who would go in and out of the Ghetto to bring food for their parents. How can you not love Jewish children? Do you know, later on when the battles began, who were those who smuggled in weapons for the Ghetto? Jewish children. And who were those who fought? Adolescents. The high command of the Warsaw Ghetto was composed of adolescents, and my friends, when I think about it, I don't understand. Where did they take the courage? Where did they take the skill? Where did they take the knowledge needed to fight in battle? Since Bar Kochba in the second century, Jewish history had no experience in military matters. And here, all of a sudden, with 500,000 Jews already killed in Treblinka, 20,000 remained in the Warsaw Ghetto. And those 20,000 produced a few hundred fighters. Now remember. Every underground, every occupied land in Europe received help, information, money, training, from London, Washington, Moscow. The only underground that did not receive *any* help from *any* quarter was the Jewish underground. And yet that underground, led by a few teenagers, managed to fight the German occupation forces, that then was the strongest military force in Europe, and the battle lasted longer than the battle of France.

Now you understand why we love Jewish children. We love them because the killers killed them. When the killers killed them, nobody paid any attention. And that's why, in every one of my novels, there is always a Jewish child, a Jewish child that I try to shield with compassion and affection and love. This is my way of saying at least to one child, "I'm going to give you a name and a roof over your head, or at least a tombstone." After all, remember, friends, that we belong to a generation, the first in our history, whose dead weren't even buried. Never did it happen to us that we couldn't even bury our dead. Heaven became our cemetery or we are their cemetery.

No, I don't understand how it happened. And the more I live, the less I will understand. But I will go on learning, and that is another lesson—although we don't understand, we must continue to learn. And although we are doomed to fail, we must continue to use words. And although we have all the right to give up on mankind, we must not give up on humankind.

In other words, and in conclusion: Friends, teachers, like you I tried to approach this problem of evil with fear and trembling, from all different categories: philosophy and psychology, theology and literature, and others and others and others, and I'm afraid that all of them prove to be pale, poor, impossible. I do not think that answers can be found in any of these categories. Only in morality can they be found. Only in morality— that means the only attitude must be a moral attitude towards the tragedy. We must choose to be moral. We must choose to be human. We must choose to be compassionate toward one another. And my friends, children of survivors, I believe there is only one area where we did not fail, and you know the area I refer to. And that is our children. We did not fail in our children. The greatest of all victories is in our children. And we are profoundly proud of you.

Chapter III

THE ABANDONMENT OF THE JEWS

David S. Wyman

The Holocaust began in June 1941, simultaneously with Germany's attack on Russia. But it was not until August 1942, 14 months later, that enough information had filtered out for Jewish leaders in the West, and Western governments, to realize that systematic extermination was underway. Even then, United States State Department officials were skeptical. They asked the American Jewish leadership not to publicize the information until it could be more fully verified. That took three more months. The State Department, by the way, did not pursue the verification with any avidity.

Finally, on November 24, 1942, Undersecretary of State Sumner Welles telephoned Rabbi Stephen Wise, the foremost American Jewish leader of that period, and asked him to come to Washington immediately. When Wise arrived in Welles's office that same day, the undersecretary confirmed the news that the Nazi plan of systematic extermination of the European Jewish people was underway. He also, at that point, approved the release of this information to the public.

Rabbi Wise immediately called a press conference. November 24, 1942, thus became a pivotal date in Holocaust history, because the terrible news of systematic extermination was available from then on to anyone in the United States, indeed to anyone in the democratic nations, who cared to know of it. It must be said, though, that the American mass media never gave Holocaust information the emphasis that it deserved. They consistently treated it as a minor news story. For example, the *New York Times* report on Rabbi Wise's press conference appeared the next day on page 10, in three little side-by-side columns of three inches — a total of nine inches of coverage. Confirmed information at that time indicated that two million had already been massacred, and the killing was going forward rapidly. Yet extermination information hardly ever reached the front pages of the American news media.

By November 1942 the Nazi extermination campaign had been underway for 17 months. Now that the information was out, one might have expected an outcry, and especially an American government effort to do what it could for rescue. Instead, it took *14 more months* to get the Roosevelt administration to act. During those 14 months, Jewish organizations struggled to force a reluctant government to confront the issue. In this effort, they received a little assistance from the organized labor movement, and very little help from Christian church leaders – a very few. Jewish groups had to carry on a two-fold campaign. They wanted to build pressure on the government for action. But in order to develop that pressure it was necessary to publicize the information because the media were not doing it. So there was a double struggle – publicizing and building pressure.

The Jewish organizations used several methods. A Day of Mourning and Prayer which took place in synagogues throughout the United States in early December 1942, was the first step. A week later, five Jewish leaders saw President Roosevelt in the White House for a half-hour conference. Petitions for government action were circulated and signed. Jewish leaders went to the State Department frequently, suggesting possible rescue steps. The Roosevelt administration did agree to issue war crimes warnings, statements threatening post-war retribution to the perpetrators. Otherwise, from Washington, there came nothing but condolences.

The United States government, especially the State Department, had two constant answers (which were really no more than excuses for inaction). First, they insisted that the only effective way to stop the slaughter was to win the war as rapidly as possible. That became a refrain during the war years. As if rescue steps could not be taken before the war ended. As if rescue could not be carried out in parallel with the winning of the war. No one, Jewish or other, requested that the war effort be compromised in any way in favor of rescue efforts. The point was that many, many things could have been done that would not have detracted from the war effort, while the war was still going on. The fact that ultimately the President did establish a rescue commission proves that these two objectives were not contradictory; it was not an either/or situation. That argument was nevertheless constantly put forward and with it came just the edge of the implication that those who cried out for rescue were somehow less patriotic than other Americans.

The second reply that came constantly from Washington was the claim that the State Department was already doing everything possible for rescue. I think the best way to illustrate the sort of action that the State Department was really taking is to display a document from the period. This is an exact photocopy of the visa application form for refugees who hoped to come into this country in that period. The form is four feet long, on two sides. A total of eight feet of intentionally obstructive red tape. It was put into use in July 1943, seven months after confirmed information of extermination had come. By then, of course, it was well known what the alternative was for the Jews who could not leave Europe.

This application form was only one of many barriers that the State Department put in the path of potential immigrants. The results were deadly. The immigration quotas available at that time would have permitted the entry of about 60,000 refugees from Europe per year. Without changing the law at all, 60,000 could have reached safety in the United States. Instead, planned State Department obstruction kept the use of those quotas to *ten percent* during the Holocaust. Six thousand per year. During the three and one-half years the United States was at war, 210,000 could have come in. Only 21,000 did. There were 189,000 unused quota slots — 189,000 lives that could have been saved and were not. One other point. It would have required no more than an order from President Roosevelt to the State Department to have opened those quotas to full use.

Despite the government's persistent excuses, pressures for action did build little by little during early 1943. Not that a large mass movement took shape. But gradually enough pressure built up, coming mainly from Jewish circles, for an impact to be felt in Washington.

In early 1943 more horrible reports came out of Europe. These stimulated further American Jewish action. The Jewish leadership turned to the use of mass meetings. These meetings were held throughout the United States in the spring of 1943. Full-page newspaper advertisements were also used, urging rescue. This was an attempt to deal with the failure of the press to bring the news to the forefront.

In addition, the State Department began to receive pressure from the British government to make some kind of move. The reason was that in England public pressures had built more substantially than in the United States in two areas. One was the Christian church leadership. The foremost British Christian church leadership, both Catholic and Protestant, had cried out very strongly for rescue directly after the news of extermination had been released. This was a major difference from what happened in the American churches, where there was close to silence on the issue. The other difference was that many important members of Parliament, probably a majority of that body, were urging action. In the United States, for many many months there was almost no response in Congress.

The British government was feeling the heat. The State Department was feeling some pressure. The result was that in April 1943 the State Department and the British Foreign Office staged a diplomatic conference on the island of Bermuda. I use the word "staged" purposely. Supposedly, the conference was held to explore what could be done about the Jewish situation. But the real purpose of the conference becomes apparent when one examines the minutes of the conference itself. The real objective of the Bermuda Conference was to dampen the pressures for action that had managed to build up. It was obvious why Bermuda was chosen as the site. Its isolated location would facilitate secrecy. It would shelter the diplomats from Jewish and other groups that might try to apply pressure. And it would allow full control of the press.

In reality, during the 12 days that it met, the Bermuda Conference developed almost no plans for rescue. It was really an exercise in finding reasons why all the suggestions that had been submitted to it could not be carried out. Yet the two governments announced afterwards that all avenues had been explored and that the United States and Britain would be doing everything possible. What they were doing would have to be kept secret, however. Publicity, they claimed, would jeopardize the rescue projects.

So, although they had planned virtually no action, the two governments now had a nearly airtight excuse for their inertia. What else could be asked? The diplomats and the experts had met, they had explored the whole issue, they had decided what should be done, and supposedly those things were now being done.

The Bermuda Conference thus served, as had been intended, to dissipate the pressures which had built up for rescue. It was, in fact, a charade, a fraud. As one of the diplomats, the leader of the British delegation admitted, in an interview 20 years later, the conference "had been a facade for inaction."

One might well ask why the American and British governments would respond in this way to the terrible tragedy of the European Jews. The basic answer is that the United States and Great Britain did not want large numbers of Jews to come out of Hitler's Europe. A few thousand a year they were willing to deal with—maybe 10,000, maybe 15,000 a year. But no tens of thousands. Whenever it appeared to the diplomats that there might conceivably be an exodus of 20 or 50 or 70 thousand, there was apprehension, indeed fear. The reason for that was that they did not see where rescued Jews could be put. No country wanted to take Jews in. That had been clear before the war. It continued to be the case even when it was known that the Jews were being annihilated. If the United States and Britain initiated steps that brought about the rescue of Jews, *they* would be responsible for finding places for them. And they saw no place to put them.

The State Department was convinced that Americans did not want any large number of Jews coming here. And it was fully aware of a strong and vocal element in Congress which was intent on keeping Jewish immigration to the United States to the barest minimum. This grew out of antisemitism that was widespread in Congress at that time. And that attitude in Congress was based on widespread antisemitism in American society during the period. All the indications are, and they include very dependable national public opinion polls, that antisemitism reached its historic peak in American society in the years of World War II, essentially from 1938 to 1944. That current in American society was reflected very definitely in Congress and in the State Department. The State Department's approach to rescue was based on its own callousness of spirit. But the most crucial factor was its belief that if Jews were allowed to immigrate in any numbers there would be a strong backlash in the Congress.

There was an excellent possibility for rescue in the summer of 1942, when mass deportations from France were occurring. Many of the children of the deportees were left behind in France. Those children were hidden. Ultimately, many of them survived, probably 5,000 to 8,000 concealed in French homes and religious institutions. There was constant fear, however, that the Nazis would hunt those children down. A relief agency, based in the United States and operating in France, asked the United States to arrange to take in 5,000 of these children and safeguard them. This the State Department agreed to, in its high water mark of generosity during the Holocaust. But State Department officials specified that the relief organization issue no publicity of the bringing of 5,000 children over here. This, of course, made it extremely difficult to raise the funds necessary to carry out the mission. The reason the State Department gave for putting the lid on publicity was that if Congress found out that as many as 5,000 Jewish children were coming here, there would be a major uproar on Capitol Hill. Yet, at this time, the quotas were virtually unused; there were approximately 55,000 available places.

Another factor was general anti-immigration attitudes. These had been very strong in the 1920s when immigration restriction was first imposed. That anti-alienism remained strong through the 1930s and was very much on the scene during the World War II period. Congress and a lot of the American population were not willing to accept the idea of sizeable immigration of any sort. For Jewish refugees there was a double barrier, because they were both aliens and Jews.

On the other side, the British did not want an exodus of Jews from Axis Europe because this would have put very heavy pressure on them to let Jews into Palestine. Britain did not want to jeopardize its policy of very limited Jewish immigration into Palestine, a policy that was set up in 1939 in order to placate the Arabs. In short, Britain and the United States, rather than trying to rescue Jews, were afraid that rescue might happen, that they might be confronted with an outflow of thousands of Jews. They were certainly not going to try to make it happen.

I have three documentary examples that I want to use to illustrate the foregoing points. The first example is in regard to a meeting held in March 1943 in Washington shortly before the Bermuda Conference. British Foreign Minister Anthony Eden was visiting the United States at that time. He was at a meeting in the White House, with President Roosevelt, American Secretary of State Cordell Hull, and a few others. Hull raised the issue of helping the 60,000 Jews in Bulgaria. Eden replied "that the whole problem of the Jews in Europe is very difficult and that we should move very cautiously about offering to take all Jews out of a country like Bulgaria. If we do that, then the Jews in the world will be wanting us to make similar offers in Poland and Germany." Eden was afraid that large numbers would be saved. These men knew well, because it had been months that the news had been available, of the alternative facing Jews who were not taken out. No one in that group questioned Eden's comments. Here we have the top leadership of the two great western democracies, with the lone exception of Winston Churchill, and no one spoke. All the others assented, by their silence, to Eden's position.

The second example is in regard to an event that came to a crisis eight months later. A plan had been proposed that might possibly bring 70,000 Jews out of Rumania and France. The official British position was to oppose it. Here is a quotation from the relevant British document:

> The British Foreign Office are concerned with the difficulties of disposing of any considerable number of Jews should they be rescued.

The British considered that it would be virtually impossible "to deal with anything like the number of 70,000 refugees."

But it was not only the British. In the third example, a State Department official put the problem this way:

> There was always the danger that the German Government might agree to turn over to the United States and to Great Britain a large number of Jewish refugees....In the event of our admission of inability to take care of these people the onus for their continued persecution would have been largely transferred from the German Government to the United States.

These three examples can be multiplied several times in the archives of both governments. Briefly put, a successful rescue program was something the British government and the State Department wished to avoid. Let me now return to events following the Bermuda Conference.

Despite the dampening effects of the Bermuda Conference, American public concern was slowly re-aroused later during 1943. What followed occurred on two separate tracks.

First, some concern finally was awakened in Congress. In November 1943 legislation was introduced in both houses calling on the President to set up a special United States government rescue agency. The objective was to get the issue out of the State Department. It looked as if this proposal would reach the floor of Congress. If it did, it would almost certainly set off an attack there on the Roosevelt administration's lack of rescue action. The attack would have come from two sides. There was a growing group of people in Congress, especially in the Senate, who were becoming more and more upset and disturbed about American inaction concerning rescue. There was another group that was always at hand and yearning to get a crack at the administration whenever it could, and that was the opponents of the Roosevelt administration, the opposition party. If the issue had come to the floor, it almost certainly would have set off a major debate which would have been very unpleasant for the Roosevelt administration. This rescue resolution put and kept strong pressure on Roosevelt in late 1943 and into January 1944. He was quite aware of the troublesome possibilities connected with that legislation.

The second track, which also developed through the last half of 1943, involved an entirely independent sequence of events. Treasury Department officials discovered in the summer of 1943 that the State Department not only had been doing nothing itself to aid Jews but had even been obstructing the attempts American Jewish organizations were making for rescue on their own, with their own limited facilities.

What brought the Treasury Department into the situation was an incident involving an attempt by a Jewish organization to initiate a rescue project. The World Jewish Congress, working from New York, applied to Washington for a license to send $25,000 to Switzerland for a relief and rescue plan. This would have been a first installment of funds for a program that looked as though it had very good hopes of success. It took from April until December of 1943 for that small request to clear the State Department. Eight months, during which time, of course, the possibilities for that program evaporated.

This incident involved the Treasury Department in the rescue issue because during World War II the transfer of any funds overseas was subject to strict licensing. The reason was the necessity to keep any money from reaching the Axis and aiding their war effort. The clearance for those fund transfer licenses had to go through two departments of government: the State Department, because it was involved in foreign affairs; and the Treasury Department, for the obvious reason that it also had a hand in the question of economic warfare. State Department officials received the request first, in April 1943, and they kicked it around until June, finding all kinds of reasons why the money should not be transferred. The underlying reason of course was fear that the plan might work and the Jews might come out.

The Treasury Department ultimately had to be consulted — there was no way around it, for that was part of the licensing procedure. In June the State Department relayed the application to the Treasury Department. The Treasury approved the license in one day. The reason that the Treasury Department did so was because it saw no problem with the license. According to the plans, the funds were to be frozen in Swiss banks until the end of the war. They would not become available in any way to anyone, including the Axis, until *after* the war. (The State Department knew this too.) It happened that there were people in Axis territory who held Axis currencies and who were willing to lend those currencies against repayment in dollars *after* the war. So the whole thing could have been financed without any possible advantage to the Axis, and therefore the Treasury Department approved it.

Yet more months passed without State Department approval of the license. Treasury officials became increasingly suspicious as the delays continued. They sensed what was going on and proceeded carefully to dig out and to compile the story of this incident and the many other instances of State Department obstruction. People from the middle level in the Treasury Department, five non-Jews and one Jew, managed through connections they had with the middle levels in the State Department to ferret out the information and to piece together almost the whole story of State Department malfeasance over the many months. They put it together in the form of a lawyer's brief and took it to the Secretary of the Treasury, Henry Morganthau.

Morganthau, who had to be pushed some before he would move on the issue, did, in January 1944, carry that evidence to President Roosevelt. Morganthau informed Roosevelt that a major scandal was about to break because this information was very likely to get out if the President did not act quickly to change his administration's policy of inaction in regard to rescue.

Morganthau also brought to Roosevelt a draft of an executive order setting up a special rescue agency. Morganthau's move, added to the continued pressure of the rescue resolution in Congress, forced Roosevelt to act. He agreed to sign the executive order. At last, late in January 1944, the President established a United States government rescue agency, which was called the War Refugee Board.

So finally, 1944 and 1945 saw an American rescue effort. But by then the hour was very late. Moreover, the War Refugee Board did not get full support from the Roosevelt government. Despite these handicaps, the War Refugee Board played a vital role, according to my best estimates, in the saving of about 200,000 Jewish lives. But it could have done very much more if three thing had happened differently: first, if the board had been formed when it should have been formed, in 1942 when extermination was first known; second, if it had received real support and cooperation from the rest of the American government and from President Roosevelt, which it did not; and third, if it had received adequate funds, which it did not. It had one million dollars in government funding — that was to pay for the administrative offices in Washington and the half-dozen people who were sent overseas to try to stimulate rescue.

As to the actual rescue operations carried on in Europe by the War Refugee Board — the funding for those actions had to be provided by Jewish private organizations, mainly the Joint Distribution Committee. The funds that went for all the rescue operations, including the work that Raoul Wallenberg did in Budapest, were paid for by Jewish American citizens through their voluntary contributions to their organizations. The Jewish people contributed 16 million dollars to rescue. That is to say, over 90 percent of what the War Refugee Board did was paid for by Jewish private citizens. An unparalleled scandal: our government established a policy, finally made rescue a national goal, and then tapped one segment, one very small segment, of the population, and said you have to pay for it. Of course, the total of 17 million dollars was not nearly enough to do the maximum job. So the War Refugee Board had to hobble along. Its achievements were unquestionably very valuable. But it certainly represented a very limited American commitment. This limited commitment came, moreover, only after more than a year of struggle to get the Roosevelt administration to act.

Chapter IV

THE MESSAGE THAT WAS DELIVERED, BUT NOT HEARD

Jan Karski

We have gathered here to commemorate what happened to the Jews forty years ago, and to draw some conclusions. Since I was an eyewitness of the Jewish Gehenna, you asked me for a statement. I accepted your invitation with gratitude. I am anxious to speak on the subject.

In order to understand how the Holocaust—a unique and incomparable phenomenon of World War II—could have happened and why we should not let humanity forget it, I suggest keeping in mind the following factors.

The world did change after World War II, but in many respects humanity has not changed. Intolerance, racism, antisemitism, hatred are still alive.

Secondly, during the war the Jews were totally helpless. They did not have their own country, government or army. They were not represented in the Allied councils. They had to depend on others. And those others were sympathetic, indifferent or hostile.

The Jews, being outside the Nazi orbit, did not have their own direct contacts with the existing Jewish underground groups in Nazi-dominated Europe. Every underground—my own Polish underground—had almost daily contacts with either the Polish government in exile or with the British government through secret radio. To this day I cannot understand that the Jews—so inventive—scattered all over the world particularly in the United States and Great Britain, failed—or were prevented from establishing—direct secret radio communications with the Jewish resistance groups. Again, they had to rely on others.

Next, the Holocaust was unique. Humanity was not prepared for it. The Jews were not prepared for it. Such a phenomenon never happened throughout history. As I heard Elie Wiesel speaking a few years ago, and he put it well, the Second World War consumed fifty million victims.

Every nation had victims. Poland lost some three million ethnic Poles. The Soviet Union lost twenty million people. But *all* Jews were victims.

Next, governments, nations, societal structures, as I understand it, have no souls. They have no conscience. They have only interests and by those interests alone they are guided. Only individuals have souls and an infinite capability to be good or bad. Spiritually, we are all schizophrenic.

The Jews were unable to contribute militarily to the victory. Military victory had the highest priority for the Allied governments: saving the Jews represented no more than a side issue to the Allies.   Thus, the governments, societal structure's and most of the organized churches failed to help the Jews.   But individuals—and there must have been thousands and thousands of them all over Europe—tried to help: workers, peasants, priests and nuns, educated and simple ones.   They could not do much—they were oppressed themselves.

We should also keep in mind that during the war, as well as today, people very often chose to be guided by self-imposed ignorance, self-controlled disbelief, soulless rationalization, self-interest, hypocrisy—if convenient.

It is within this framework that I want to tell you my story.

During most of the war I was used by the Polish Underground as a secret courier.   In 1939, from Poland to France.   In 1940, from France back to Poland.   Then again to France.   Then to Great Britain.   At that time I was young and strong. I knew languages. I knew Europe.

In the summer of 1942, I had been scheduled to go to London on my fourth secret mission.   Approximately in September, the Delegate of the Polish government-in-exile, residing in Warsaw, Cyryl Ratajski, informed me that the leaders of two Jewish resistance organizations—Socialist and Zionist—learned about my mission and requested permission to use me, if I were willing.   I agreed.   Soon, they established contact with me, identifying themselves by their functions.   The post-war literature seems to agree the Socialist (*Bund*) leader must have been Leon Finer.   As to the Zionist, as far as I know, no definite identification has been established.

The Jewish leaders gave me several desperate messages to the Polish government as well as to those Allied leaders whom I would be able to reach.   With their help and secret contacts I succeeded twice in entering the Jewish ghetto in Warsaw.   Disguised as an Estonian militiaman, I was able to see the concentration camp of Belzec.   What I saw and heard eventually I revealed in my book *Story of a Secret State*, published in the United States and Great Britain in 1944—during the war.

The messages I carried which I did deliver in London, and a few months later in Washington, were marked by despair and utter helplessness.   The Nazis had decided to exterminate all Jews in Europe before the war's end and regardless of its outcome.   The Jews were helpless.   They could not rely on the Poles who might be able to save some individuals but who could not save or help the Jews. The Polish Jews placed historical responsibility on the Allied governments to do so.

Let the Allied governments inform the German people through radio, the BBC, of what is being done to the Jews. Let millions of leaflets be dropped over Germany describing the ghettos, death camps, names of the Nazi perpetrators, statistics, details, so that no German would be able to say that he did not know. Let the Allies publicly ask the German people to exercise pressure on their government to stop murdering the Jews and to give evidence that such a pressure had been exercised.

If the German nation did not react and their government continued its monstrous and unprecedented action, let the Allies make a public announcement that unprecedented retaliation, not required by military strategy, would follow. Certain objects of particular value to Germany would be destroyed through air bombings. Each mission, before and after, would contain a public message directed to the German nation that the bombing was in retaliation for what the Nazis were doing to the Jews as well as an announcement that bombing would continue as long as persecution of the Jews continued.

Let the Allied governments offer haven to those Jews who escaped from the Nazi terror and prevail upon neutral countries to do likewise.

As for the Jewish leaders in England, and particularly in the United States, I was to tell them that the funds which the Jewish resistance received through the Delegate of the Polish government were totally insufficient. Hard currency or gold was needed to bribe the Nazi officials so that they would let some Jews leave the ghettos. Original but blank passports were needed. The corrupted Nazi officials would close their eyes and let the Jews leave Poland — for money or gold, of course. Money was needed to pay the Polish families who hid or were willing to hide the Jews. The Poles were in dire need themselves.

I carried also a microfilmed report concealed in a regular house key. A part of the report dealt with the Jewish situation in Poland. The report was prepared by Professor Ludwik Widerszal, Professor Stanislaw Herbst and Henryk Wolinski — all members of the underground Home Army.

I left Poland at the beginning of November 1942 and reached London three weeks later passing Berlin, Brussels, Paris, Lyons, Perpignan, the Pyrenees Mountains (on foot), Barcelona, Madrid, Algeciras, Gibraltar and then by air to London.

According to the British archives inspected and published many years after the war by prominent British historian Martin Gilbert (in his book *Auschwitz and the Allies*), the report called "Karski's Report" was handed on November 26, 1942 to the Deputy Foreign Secretary, Sir Richard Low.

Then I began my oral reports. I reported in London to four members of the British War Cabinet: Anthony Eden, Lord Cranbron, Arthur Geenwood and Hugh Dalton as well as to Lord Shelborne, who secretly supervised all European resistance organizations. I also informed several members of the House of Commons.

In the middle of 1943, I was dispatched to the United States where I made my report to President Franklin D. Roosevelt, Secretary of State Cordell Hull, Secretary of War Henry Stimson, Attorney General Francis Biddle, Apostolic Delegate Cardinal Cicognani, Archbishops Spellman, Stritch and Mooney. The Jewish leaders whom I informed were President of the American Jewish Congress, Nahum Goldmann, Justice of the Supreme Court, Felix Frankfurter, Walter Lippman, George Sokolski and many others.

Both in London and Washington I was asked to pass the information to various individuals from the local intelligence community. Since I was scheduled to return to Poland on my fifth secret mission, I functioned under an assumed name of "Jan Karski." Upon my return from Washington to London in September 1943, Stanislaw Mikolajczyk, who succeeded Gen. Sikorski as Prime Minister, reversed the decision. I had become too well known in the United States. Nazi radio mentioned me as a "Bolsehevik agent on the payroll of American Jews." As during World War II, so by the way today: Americans talk too much.

I was asked by the organization of this conference to describe the reactions to my Jewish report.

Foreign Secretary Eden—I saw him twice—listened attentively to my general report concerning the situation in Poland and activities of our Underground. When I came to the Jewish part, he interrupted me and said: "Karski's report has already reached us. The matter will take its proper course." Then he asked me many questions; none of them concerned the Jews. Eventually I learned that on January 18, 1943, at the Interallied Council, Polish Acting Foreign Minister (still alive in London) Count Edward Raczynski reported the content of my Jewish mission and Jewish demands. To every point, in the name of His Majesty's government, Eden said "no." Great Britain already had 100,000 refugees. There was no room for more. The Allies must concentrate on the military defeat of Germany. His Majesty's government will not allow side issues to interfere. A negative attitude was also held by the American delegation on a purely legal basis. The proposed plan to rescue the Jews did not fit into the regulations of the immigration quota in the United States.

During my second contact with Eden, he introduced me to Lord Selborne, the one who supervised all the underground anti-Nazi movements. His reaction—very frank, very responsive. But when I mentioned the hard currency, he became almost outraged. No government, no political leader, would approve of such a plan. "If we sent hard currency or gold probably we would be able to keep it secret during the war, but eventually it would become known, and then no one among us would take the risk to be accused by our own public opinion that we were financing Hitler with gold and hard currency with which he would buy military equipment or raw materials from neutral countries," he said. He was sympathetic toward the Jews. He encouraged me to talk, to speak, to contact people. But he also told me a story of the First World War. He remembered that during the First World War there were rumors in Europe that the German soldiers liked to play, seizing babies by the head and crashing their skulls against walls. Of course His Majesty's government knew that those rumors were not true, but they didn't do anything to deny them. And then, "Mr. Karski. You are doing wonderful work informing people what is happening to the Jews. We stand behind you. We will help you." No, I did not ask His Lordship why he had told me that story. This did not belong to me. I was a courier, a little guy. I was not supposed to ask questions — only to answer them.

Justice Frankfurter, whom I had met at the Polish Embassy in August, was introduced to me by the Polish Ambassador Jan Ciechanowski. The men were close friends. Frankfurter was unimpressive, a little pompous, but brilliant. Before I started he asked me, "Do you know who I am?" "Yes, sir, I know." "Do you know that I am a Jew?" "Yes, sir. Mr. Ambassador told me about it." "Being so," he said, "tell me what happens to the Jews in your country. There are many conflicting rumors about it."

To Justice Frankfurter I made a fuller, longer and more precise report on the Jews than to anyone else. He asked me some questions; I don't remember which ones. Then, there was silence. He got up and walked across the room, in silence. Then, he stood in front of me and said — this conversation I remember well. "Mr. Karski," he said, "a man like me, talking to a man like you, must be totally frank. So I say I am unable to believe you." The Polish Ambassador broke in, "Felix! You don't mean it. You cannot tell him that he is a liar to his face when you know he was checked and rechecked. He is telling the truth. Felix!" Justice Frankfurter answered, "Mr Ambassador, I did not say that this young man is lying. I said that I am unable to believe him. There is a difference." No, I did not ask him whether he was sincere.

Then I saw Shmul Zygelbojm in London. He was antagonistic, unpleasant. He didn't seem to like me, I don't know for what reasons. Perhaps he resented that I was not Jewish. He was suspicious, excited. At the end of my report, he burst out "I am doing everything. What do they want from me? I cannot do anything more. You didn't tell me anything I didn't know. I know more than you told me." Then, hurt and tired as I was, I gave in to him. "The Jews in Warsaw asked me to tell the Jewish leaders in the West," I said. "Let them not tell us that they cannot do anything more. Let them go to the offices of their governments. Let them ask for help for us. If there is no definite answer, let them stand at the doors of those offices in the street. Let them refuse water. Let them refuse food. Let them die publicly, in the streets, in view of all humanity. Perhaps that will shake the conscience of the world. We are dying here."

He jumped running from one end of the room to another. "The world is mad, mad. If I do such a thing, they will send two policemen, they will send me to a psychiatric unit, they will not let me die in the street. What to do? What to do? How can I do, if I do not know what to do? Madness, madness."

On May 11, 1943, at the time that the Jewish war waged against the Third Reich in the Jewish ghetto of Warsaw came to an end, he killed himself.

Having reported to the highest Catholic prelates and the Apostolic Delegate, on each occasion I fell on my knees and kissed the holy ring. Each of them blessed me. Nothing more.

I reported to H. G. Wells, the famous author. He listened, asked some questions. After I concluded my Jewish report, he wondered loudly, "What is the reason that in every country where Jews reside, sooner or later antisemitism emerges?" He asked me whether I thought about it.

President Roosevelt impressed me with his majesty—I saw in him a master of humanity. I was awed by his power. He asked me several questions. Essentially he was interested in political events, but he did ask me some questions on my Jewish report as well. He didn't say anything specific except that "the guilty ones will be punished for their crimes. You will tell your leaders that we shall win this war." Roosevelt was my hero. I admired him. Great reformer. I left him, however, with some mixed feelings.

Years later, not a very long time ago, I learned that perhaps I was wrong. John Pehle (his name perhaps is familiar to you) gave an interview to the *San Francisco Chronicle* on October 29, 1981. In that interview he stated, I quote: "Karski's mission to Roosevelt did succeed in changing overnight Jewish policy from one of indifference at best to affirmative action. The President ordered an immediate creation of the War Refugee Board. I was named director. I cannot say the Refugee Board accomplished any miracles, but it wasn't for lack of trying. By and large, the American efforts were too little too late."

I know that the Board began to function in February 1944, but I reported the Jewish part of my mission to the American Ambassador in London, Anthony Drexel Biddle, one year before, in January or February, 1943. What happened with that report? Had he reported to the President? This is a good subject for research, to check in the American archives.

Then I started, as I mentioned, reporting to the second string of dignitaries, mostly intelligence officers, diplomats. Their arguments invariably represented a rationalization of passivity. "Mass reprisals as requested by the Jews would mean an open and official adoption of the Nazi policy of collective responsibility. We cannot engage in this kind of policy."

Another argument: Allied pilots, when ordered to fly over Germany to drop leaflets, or carry out retaliatory bombing of non-military nature, may resent it. They might suffer severe losses. They fight for their own countries, not for some particular segments of population.

Another argument: British public opinion might wonder whether the Nazi propaganda that the war is being waged by the Jews is true. Psychologically, it might be risky to engage in such activities.

Another argument: Nazi-dominated European nations may resent retaliatory bombings in behalf of the Jews. Why has the persecution of the Jews been singled out? Every nation is suffering. Oh, I remember. "Your own people, Mr. Karski, might resent it too. We cannot engage in such an action."

Next argument: We are receiving many reports from many countries about many aspects of life in Nazi-dominated Europe. Not all the reports, however, are credible. Not all the reports can be verified. We are not sure whether your report is verifiable.

Another argument: The war is being waged on many fronts, and it is up to us not to weaken any of those fronts. We have to take under consideration all factors, and we are waging this war to bring freedom to *all* nations of Europe, not only Jews.

These are the arguments and the individuals I remember forty years after. So what should we do now? I am not wise enough and I am not big enough to have suggestions. I don't know. The world is so strange. So unpredictable. You never know what will happen next. And people, they are so good, they are so bad. You never know what they will do to you.

People like you in this room, all of you, are engaged in activities not to allow the governments, the nations, the individuals to forget what happened to the Jews forty years ago, to remind them again and again of what happened. For this kind of activity, every decent human being must have respect for you, must be grateful to you. You are trying to redeem humanity.

Chapter V

FORTY YEARS AFTER: A DELIBERATE MISUNDERSTANDING

Harry James Cargas

I want to begin by addressing you as "my dear artists." When Franklin and Marcia Littell invited me to speak at this conference, I asked them if I could be permitted to deliberately misunderstand the topic. (Franklin said "Why not, you've been deliberately misunderstanding things for years!") The "forty years after" to which I'd like to address myself is forty years after now—I want to ask what it is that people will be talking about in the year 2025 that we were so blind to in the year 1985. One of the things I dread is the prospect of a Jan Karski getting up in 2025 and telling us the kinds of things that he told us last night.

I have here a "story" from *The New York Times* from July 28, 1942. This story is, revealingly, not on page one but on page eight. The first headline reads "Yugoslavs Driving the Axis from Bosnia." Then there's a secondary headline "Guerillas Rout Italians and Cause State of Siege in Zagreb, London Hears." The third headline is this: "Nazis Said to Plan Wiping Out of 600,000 in the Ghetto." The fate of 600,000 Jews in the Warsaw Ghetto begins to be acknowledged in the *ninth* paragraph of the news story. One of the questions I'm asking is, What's inside the Philadelphia *Inquirer* today?

As was mentioned, I'm editing a new journal, *Holocaust and Genocide Studies,* and in the credo of the periodical I point out that Max Brod makes the distinction between two kinds of suffering, noble and ignoble. The former is the kind we experience when we have no control over it as a human race, such as earthquakes, or tornados. Ignoble suffering occurs—and there is no blame on the victim implied—when people experience pain which can be prevented, such as the starving children in Ethiopia are being plagued by even as we meet here. The journal will focus on ignoble suffering; asking not only what we can do to relieve, but to prevent future genocides everywhere.

One of the attitudes that we need to have drawn to our attention is the distinction that John Coultre makes in a new book, *Outliving the Self*, in which he reminds us of the two views towards life that people hold: the *me* attitude and the *beyond me* philosophy. He says that in the 1970s professional observers of American society were concerned about an increasing "incapacity or unwillingness on the part of its citizens to identify with the future – to be interested in offspring and willing to sacrifice for them, to leave the site of one's life in better shape than it was found, to feel one has something of value for succeeding generations." Coultre shows himself to be in agreement with Christopher Lasch who wrote that "We are fast losing the sense of historical continuity, the sense of belonging to a succession of generations originating in the past and stretching into the future." The key here is, of course, responsibility. Coultre identifies the Ericksonian concept of generativity which he modifies somewhat and defines as "a desire to invest one's substance in forms of life and work that will outlive the self."

Perhaps the most obvious reference to be made here is to the tobacco industry, people who are making a living by trying to poison my children, my grandchildren and of course the great grandchildren whom I will never see. The tobacco trade press describes the Third World as receptive and potentially lucrative. This industry spent, in 1977 alone, millions of dollars in advertising its murderous product throughout the planet. Much of this was done in the poorer countries where no surgeon-generals warnings need be printed. Often it takes only a modest bribe to certain officials to eliminate such obstacles. Smoking is not only associated by image manipulators with sexual prowess and sophistication; in some nations it is promoted as a symbol of a woman's independence. You can show those around you, progressive woman that you are, that you are free of the traditional restraints with which your society has shackled you by having a rebellious cigarette in your hand. (By the way, the resources used to make profits in tobacco overseas are borrowed by companies from Third World banks – which are thus helping to destroy the health of their own people!)

Acid rain? It is rapidly becoming the most serious environment issue of our time. We talk about responsibility: What responsibility do Americans have for acid rain falling on Canadians? What responsibility do people in the United Kingdom, France, Italy and Spain have – who are protected from their own acid rains by south-westerly winds – toward those in nations located downwind? Officials in West Germany, another great offender, were not very interested in the problem until they found out it was having a ruinous impact on the Black Forest. Now they are taking some steps to improve the situation.

We are talking about what I call vegicide or ecocide, but it's really international suicide. So I thought we might just look at today's paper for a moment or two and see what the *Inquirer* tells us. Here: "34 Lebanese Die in Israeli Raid on Shiite Village." "Tolerating Mob Lawyers" is criticized. "Iraq attacks Tehran for the first time." "Vietnamese Repulse Cambodian Assault by Recapturing Rebels Last Big Base." Or we can look at the New York *Times*. Here are stories from around the world that appear on page five and just get short notice: "Black Boycott in Johannesburg Area." "Shultz and Mexicans Discuss Border Concerns." "Seven Bombs Explode in Two Portuguese Cities." These are hardly the kinds of stories we hear on television which, we are told by the promoters, gives us *all* the news. There is another story on Rev. Douglas Roth, the Lutheran pastor who asked yesterday if he could, for his own protection, tape the heresy proceeding against him so that when he made an appeal he could have some accurate record of what was being said—but this was denied him.

One of the things I do which Professor Littell was gracious enough *not* to mention in his generous introduction of me is that I write a sports column; I think I'm only the only Holocaust scholar who does that. And I am writing a book on the morality of sports, so I read the sports pages from the same point of view. (We are talking about degree now.) Let me make a brief reference to this morning's sports pages. Yannick Noah, the French tennis star, played for France in a Davis Cup match against Paraguay, and punched out a referee. He was joined in this brawl by a teammate. Another little item: two Clemson coaches plead guilty to prescribing steroids for their athletes. Then there's an article on hockey. A philosophy of one of the team owners is expressed: you can't beat them on the ice, if you can't beat them in the alley. (So in my column I annually select hockey's All-Goon Squad composed of players I think could join the Ohio National Guard and beat on Kent State students when each season ends.)

Yesterday's paper: Khomeini is talking about retaliating. When we think about the Ayatollah, we are reminded of those terrible attacks on those people of peace, the Baha is in his country—the Jews of Iran today—who are persecuted only because they are Bahai. They are forced to carry special identity cards. Many are killed or imprisoned, and those who are not are hounded by Iranian officials. For example, Bahais who were in government work—and previously they were many because of the Bahai stress on education (now of course none are in the government)—are being forced to pay back all of their earnings from such jobs.

The Middle East in general: I wonder how many of you have had the opportunity to read not Mao's *Red Book* but Col. Quadhafi's *Green Book* in which he solves all the main problems of the world. It's funny until we realize what he's doing with this kind of thing. He also has *Green Book, Part Two*, "The Solution to the Economic Problem." It's so simple for him; the answers are so easy. And they are right here before us. All that you have to do is write to the Libyan U. N. office, they'll be happy to send you copies free.

The crackdown in Poland, Cypress tension, American farmers, the ongoing story of racism in this country, the Pittsburgh minister who is being disciplined because he dares to preach that the Gospel has something to do with social justice, Cambodia, Vietnam—what do we have to say about all of this—and so much more. And Ireland? A very well-known Catholic priest in this country, with a very Irish name, told me that when he went to Ireland recently he kept hearing stories about a Protestant British family that had moved into the neighborhood not far from where he was staying with friends. His host was always reviling the newcomers. At one point my priest-friend was being driven by the houses of the despised British. "Father, that's where *they* live." So tired of hearing all of this bad mouthing of Protestants, the American suggested, "Well, why don't you try to convert them?" The driver pulled over to the side of the street, looked at his passenger and said, in a steely tone, "Father, we'd rather see them rot in hell." This is the kind of condition that we may be vaguely aware of, but I wonder if we'll be reaping the harvest of such an attitude forty years from now.

South Korea? Those of us who served in the Korean War justifiably ask ourselves: What was that all about? Are we talking about democracy here or are we speaking of protecting certain peoples' political positions? What about the Silesian fantasy we read of a couple of weeks ago in a West German periodical, picturing the West German army gloriously sweeping through an Eastern Europe in which "The overwhelming part of the populace greeted the Germans as liberators from Soviet imperialism." *Somebody is thinking like that!*

Keep an eye on Indonesia. Ninety percent of its 160,000,000 are Moslem. But it is not a Moslem state, and you know whom that is going to offend. Much of Islam is on a collision course with fundamentalism in this 13,000 island nation full of potentially explosive ethnic pockets. And remember that we lived through a purge in Indonesia where 600,000 people were killed because they didn't believe the right way. And what of Hindu fundamentalism running rampant in some parts of India and boding ill for tolerance, particularly where Sikhs are concerned? This unrest could spread to Pakistan and even beyond.

Ethiopia is perhaps the most dramatic image we have currently of ignoble suffering. At a World Future Society Conference some years ago in Washington, I heard the late Herman Kahn, who had the ears of several administrations as a recognized expert, say that the hunger problem is solved. It's over. But what we have to realize, in the real world, is it is solved because we write off Haiti and we write off Chad and we write off Pakistan and we don't waste our resources there because those are insoluble problems—let them go.

South Africa rules Namibia against several U. N. resolutions. Let me point out a book to you by Jonathan Kwitny entitled *Endless Enemies: The Making of an Unfriendly World* where the author proves—among many, many other things—that in the name of free markets the United States goes around rigging international markets. Now it's easy, of course, for us to pick on the United States. We focus on ourselves because, perhaps, we have more information; or even more possibly because the disappointment in the gap between ideals and practice is so great. We could, and elsewhere I do, focus on the Soviet Union as well. I am reminded of something I heard William Sloane Coffin indicate recently at a conference on sanctuary for Central American refugees when he mentioned that Russia is the only nation in the world surrounded by hostile Communist countries. At this sanctuary meeting in Tucson it was very moving to see some eighty people who were going around with kerchiefs covering their lower faces throughout the five days because they were absolutely fearful of being identified. Our State Department has admitted that we have signed a treaty that said we would grant asylum to those who suffered from political persecution. However, our officials say, these people are *not* fleeing political repression but rather they are running away from starvation, from poverty. Therefore it is concluded that we have no obligation to them—even where we are morally certain than these non-politicos may be killed if deported back to their homelands. Do you know what some men in the U. S. Immigration and Naturalization Service are *doing in your name?* They are not only arresting illegal aliens (Elie Wiesel insists there is no such thing as an illegal human being), they are beating them, torturing them. Recently a piece appeared in the paper about Cuban refugees being encouraged to apply for citizenship here in the U. S. Some officials are amazed because not many of them are applying. I'll tell the officials why. These poor people are frightened that when they apply they'll be turned over to the Immigration and Naturalization Service and not only will they be beaten, but that their names will be turned back to their governments so that the families back home can be persecuted. That, ladies and gentlemen, is what is actually happening to Latin refugees.

Child abuse. Drugs.

So what does a professor of literature say about that? A professor of literature says that we have to read more literature, actually. Those of us who were reading Pablo Neruda's poetry were not surprised when Allende was elected president in Chile. The State Department was; our government was. When Richard Nixon was reevaluating our Latin American policy he sent Nelson Rockefeller to 17 nations in 14 days. Rocky spoke to the dictators and returned with good news: the people were all happy down there. I said give *me* Rockefeller for 17 days. I'll lock him in a room with 17 books by Neruda, Ernesto Cardenal, Gabriel Garcia Marquez, Carlos Fuentes, Miguel Angel Asturias, Octavio Paz, Julio Cortazar and writers such as they. Then he'll know a lot more about what South Americans think than he learned from his gilded trip, and more than our military spokespeople are able to report.

(Not all military are blind, of course. When the U. S. troops landed in the Dominican Republic the *first* time in this century, some eighty years ago, General Smedley Butler, in answer to a reporter's query about the mission, said, "We're here to make this place safe for the boys from the First National City Bank."   South Americans haven't forgotten that truism.)

And we can read others.   Czechoslovakian novelists like Ludvik Vaculik (who wrote jokes into the Czeck Constitution which lasted so brief a time before Soviet retribution) and Milan Kundera.   Kundera, among other themes, insists on the need for memory.   His novel, *The Book of Laughter and Forgetting* begins with this memorable episode.   We read of a Communist leader who addresses an outdoor crowd in Prague in the winter.   An assistant gives the bare-headed leader his own fur hat to help keep the leader warm.   Photos of the speech appeared everywhere, in papers, books, on posters.   Some years later, the assistant—the hat lender—was tried for treason and hanged.   The propaganda section of the Party airbrushed the assistant from every photo and poster.   Where he stood is only a blank wall.   But the fur hat is still on the leader's head to this day—and that true story tells so much.   What about us?   What's being airbrushed out for us?   What are we in fact airbrushing out ourselves?

One of the great works of literature, appropriate for our time, is a play by Henrik Ibsen, *An Enemy of the People*.   This is a drama about a scientist who discovers that the basis for his community's wealth, mineral baths advertised as curative, are not only not healthful but are in fact harmful.   He is designated as an enemy of the people because he is going to hurt the economy.   Never mind what the waters are doing to people who come in; never mind what tobacco does to the smokers.   I think, my dear artists who are gathered here, each of us must be an "enemy of the people" when the people are in favor of, or indifferent to, death.

I teach a course in Prison Literature at Webster University, or what is sometimes called Lazarene Literature.   We begin with the letters of St. Paul and go to the work of John Bunyan, Malcolm Braly (whose *On The Yard* is surely the finest novel of prison experience), Martin Luther King's "Letters from Birmingham Jail," the Holocaust memoirs of Elie Wiesel, Alexander Donat, Andre Stein, Charlotte Delbo and so many others.   We have so many authors in this community of suffering: Solzhenitsyn in the USSR, Kim Chi Ha in Korea, Ali Taygun in Turkey, George Mangakis in Greece and those who actually found religion while incarcerated like Mihajlo Mihajlov in Yugoslavia.   But there is another kind of literature too: we get the inarticulate characters of Samuel Beckett who can't seem to make utterances about this world any more.   Or the philosophically ab-surd literature coming particularly out of France.   For example, there's the humorous work of fiction, *The Flight of Icarus* by Raymond Queneau.   It begins with a novelist writing at his desk.   The doorbell rings, he goes out of the room to answer it, and the characters he was writing about jump off the page and they interact with him and the people who just came in through the door.   When we see how silly that is, we need to have brought to our attention that we were willing to grant that novelist who was sitting there a certain *r*eality, but not the characters he was creating. Yet how real was that original character?   How real is the author, Raymond Queneau, we are led to ask. How real are *you* dear listener? Alain Robe-Grillet is a novelist who gives us a plot and takes it away. Halfway through he shows us events in another perspective and when we finish a novel we don't know if any of that took place or not. We are reminded from several points of view of what happened during the Second World War—when even an Elie Wiesel can ask, "Did those things really happen?" Or when the American Kurt Vonnegut, at a certain place in *Breakfast of Champions*, enters the novel and frees his characters (some who appeared in several of his books). He will never use Killgor Trout and Eliot Rosewater again. What's real and what isn't? Do we need memory?

Recall, for a moment what I said earlier about "me" and "beyond me" attitudes, philosophies of life. Now let me point out that no important existentialist character, those men and women so morbid about the absurdity of life, those who contemplate suicide throughout their works (and who do kill themselves in the dramas of de Motherland, for instance), not one, in any of the literature, has a child. No children, no sense of the future, no responsibility.

I also teach Japanese literature in translation. Probably 25 of the 40 major fiction writers of this century in Japan have committed suicide. I think that a significant reason is that their dedication and devotion to their own tradition is being undermined by an increasing attraction to encroaching Western technology and values. I went to Japan on R and R during the Korean War and was deeply impressed in Tokyo, on the Ginza, when Japanese businessmen would greet each other with the traditional deep bow which means "I bow to the God within you." What a beautiful recognition. I went back 15 years later and it has become industrialized bowing: get in as many bends forward as you could in as short a time as possible so you get on to the serious work of making a living. It was a sad transformation.

Then there is Alberto Moravia in Italy, the only author ever to be honored in that nation by having a uniform edition of his complete writings published while still living. A novel like *Women of Rome*—about a person whose profession is selling love—shows how this postwar generation cannot love. That is a major theme, whether certain authors intend it or not, in most of contemporary Italian fiction of any literary merit.

I'm reminded of Graham Greene's *The End of the Affair* in which, at the end of the story, the so-called atheist, when he loses the Christian woman he loves because of her devotion to her faith, has nothing to do but shake his fist at the God who had done this to him, the God he refused to acknowledge existed.

And I think of art, my dear artists, as a protest against death. We are all called to be artists, in our work specifically, in our lives more generally. This has been a non-scholarly assessment and that's deliberate. I sometimes think—and I say this to *you* thoughtfully and with love—that sometimes it is too easy to be a scholar. Sometimes it's too easy to address the serious problems of the world from the stacks of the library where it's safe and clean. It was Dietrich Bonhoeffer who urged those of us who could, to get our hands dirty. David Soul's father, the Rev. Robert Solberg, saw it straight when he talked about the "maddening ambiguity" of the situation in Pittsburgh. Wouldn't it be nice if the resolution were so clear that it would be easy to find out which side of every issue we should be on. We *must* get our hands dirty. Death is out there for all of us to see. I repeat, we need to become enemies of the people, where the people collaborate with death. Or forty years from now *we* will be seen as the indifferent, as the lukewarm, as those who will be spewed forth by the Judgment of History or perhaps by the Judgment of God.

Chapter VI

THE SUBVERSION OF JUSTICE: LESSONS IN LEGAL ETHICS

J. Willard O'Brien

In a newsletter written by Franklin Littell last August (1984), Dr. Littell stated several axioms he believes have emerged from the study of the Holocaust. One of these axioms is this: Societies that do not seek to expand the liberty, the dignity and the integrity of the human person do not remain static: they go bad....For the comparatively few democratic countries to retain their commitment to liberty, minimally there must be education for tolerance toward those of different belief and practices....

In connection with his axioms, Dr. Littell also noted this:

Item: The Holocaust was dependent, for its planning and supervision and efficient execution, upon university men and women. The modern university cut loose from ethics and religion and even commitment to life and the human measure, has become an engine for producing large numbers of technically competent barbarians. Axiom: The reconstruction of the university is imperative if comparable disasters are to be averted.

When I was asked to participate on this panel, Lessons in Professional Ethics, I began to think about the connection, if any, between Dr. Littell's conclusions and the actual training and practice of the American lawyer. I believe that, for the average American lawyer, the Holocaust has changed nothing.

Pertinent here are a few observations made by a man trained in the law at a superb law school, a man who later in life served as a friend and confidant of a President of the United States, a man who himself sought unsuccessfully that same high office: the man, the Honorable Sargent Shriver; the president, John Fitzgerald Kennedy.

Mr. Shriver spoke in the Rockefeller Chapel at the University of Chicago on Sunday, October 22, 1978. His words showed surprise, sadness and perhaps resignation:

> I went to Yale Law School in 1938 naively expecting to study about justice...what was right and wrong; what ought to be done to improve society; how to extend the writ of law to overcome the inequities of life. Did I get a shock! The Professors told me the law had little or nothing to do with justice. What the judge ate for breakfast had more to do with his rulings than legal precedents....Oliver Wendell Holmes' famous dicta were almost holy writ. Holmes had written concerning the law that there was 'no brooding omnipresence in the sky' – no law that transcended the particularities of cases which were to be decided on pragmatic, social mores grounds.
>
> When persons in our society reach a certain level in business, law, medicine, politics, education and other professions, many of the problems they face are moral problems. For the person who becomes President of the United States nearly all the problems are moral problems. Rarely, if ever, does the President lack for military advice, scientific advice, financial advice, medical advice, female advice, Chicano advice, Black advice, or diplomatic advice. He just can't get the advice he needs the most.

Have things changed? Mr. Shriver went to the Yale Law School in 1938. In 1978, 40 years later, Roger C. Crampton, then Dean of the Cornell Law School, wrote an article entitled "The Ordinary Religion of the Law School Classroom." [1] As the title suggests, Dean Crampton was concerned about the "fundamental value assumptions of law professors and law students." He listed the tenets of the ordinary religion of the American law school classroom as follows:

> (1) a skeptical attitude toward generalizations; (2) an instrumental approach to law, and lawyering; (3) a 'tough-minded' and analytical attitude toward legal tasks and professional roles; and (4) a faith that man, by the application of his reason and the use of democratic processes, can make the world a better place.

Let's take a very brief look at what those tenets lead to.

The first of those tenets, namely "a skeptical attitude toward generalizations," mandates the denial of the existence of God or, at least, the denial of the relevance of God to the legal system. Under that ingredient: "There is no 'brooding omnipresence' from which principles or rules can be derived." "From a realistic standpoint, law is merely what officials of the law do."

As for the second tenet, namely, the instrumental approach to law taken in law schools, the result is that "since the lawyer is engaged in the implementation of the values of others—a client or a government agency or the general society—he need not be concerned directly with value question." Because of the tough-minded, analytical attitude adopted by law professors, i. e., the third tenet, "two models of professional behavior are presented to law students: the 'hired gun' and the 'social engineer'....The hired gun gets his goals from the client he serves; the social engineer either prefabricates his own goals or gets them from the interests he serves."

According to Dean Crampton not much has changed in the 40 years that elapsed since Sargent Shriver first arrived at the Yale Law School. Not much has changed since 1978 either.

Professor Harold J. Berman, the James Barr Ames Professor of Law at the Harvard Law School, has thought about the evolution of the law into an instrument of the powerful. After recognizing that some men and women believe that God is the source of our basic rights, Professor Berman writes:

> This was undoubtedly the view of the men who framed the Constitution, including the first amendment. Thomas Jefferson, who was perhaps the most freethinking of the founding fathers, said in 1801, in his first message as President, that 'the liberties of a nation [cannot] be thought secure when we have removed their only firm basis, a conviction in the minds of the people that their liberties are the gift of God.' Jefferson was an ardent advocate of freedom of every kind of opinion, but he also believed that despite all diversity, there was a common core of religious belief that was essential to preserve peace and order in society.[2]

Things are now different. Professor Berman writes further that:

> In the past two generations the public philosophy of America has shifted radically from a religious to a secular theory of law, from a moral to a political or instrumental theory....Rarely, if ever, does one hear it said that law is a reflection of an objective justice or of the ultimate meaning or purpose of life. Usually it is thought to reflect, at best, the community's sense of what is expedient, and

more commonly, the more or less arbitrary will of the law-maker.[3]

If I were a survivor that would frighten me. I know that because it frightens me even now.

In our country we have public law schools—public in the sense that they are part of public universities—and private law schools. Both kinds of schools teach professional ethics. But what is "professional ethics" concerned about? Mostly things that have nothing at all to do with the lessons that Franklin Littell and I believe should be learned from the Holocaust.

Professional ethics, the subject, is concerned, primarily, with the rules that govern the conduct of lawyers in dealing with clients, other lawyers, judges and, infrequently, the public: do not steal, avoid conflicts of interest, and so forth. Such rules can be helpful in trying to improve the profession, but they have little or nothing to do with what we should have learned from the murder of six million Jews.

And when we look at some of the rules, some people react negatively. That is, some believe that the legal profession's own code of conduct is barbarous, at least in part. Listen to these words written by a psychologist-philosopher for those people whose job it is to determine whether someone should be permitted to become a lawyer. The writer questioned whether we should even try to determine whether would-be lawyers are "of good moral character." Why? Listen to what he wrote. Perhaps I should add that he wrote in broad strokes deliberately to provoke, but he wrote what he believes. I quote: "Now one can debate at length what makes someone a morally good person." Most of the discussions have focused on this issue. He goes on further to say:

> All these debates are beside the point, however, [if morality is not relevant]. If it is not necessary to be a morally good person in order to be a good lawyer, if indeed it is sometimes a hindrance, then moral fitness tests are pointless....
> The recent literature on the professional responsibilities of lawyers attempts to work out a professional ethics for lawyers. In so doing many legal scholars have further challenged the assumption that a good lawyer is a good person. Perhaps the most famous (or infamous) example of this is Monroe Freedman. In a groundbreaking article he argued that a lawyer must put his client on the stand knowing that he intends to commit perjury. By ordinary moral standards it is wrong to lie and to help others to lie. Yet Freedman's lawyer would permit it and perhaps by his silence facilitate his client's lying.

> Ordinarily it is wrong to harm innocent people. But if a
> defense attorney can discredit a truthful rape victim's tes-
> timony, because she is emotionally distraught, the Code of
> Professional Responsibility would enjoin to do so.
> These examples can be multiplied, qualified and ques-
> tioned....
> No doubt many would like to dismiss these examples as
> aberrations, exceptions to the rule that good lawyers are
> good people. But I do not think they are exceptions. For
> the roots of the lawyer's moral obligation is in his duty to
> represent his client's interest zealously within the limits of
> the law. However one quibbles over the qualification
> 'zealously,' the point remains that the primary constraint
> on the lawyer's action is the law and not morality — certain-
> ly not his own morality, nor the community's morality, nor
> any general or ordinary morality, except insofar as these
> have been enacted into law.

At this point I might note that I am a lawyer and I believe that
lawyers are a positive force for good in the society within which I live. I
might also point out that we are, at this juncture, talking about trial
lawyers engaged in the adversary process. American lawyers, or, perhaps I
should say, some of them, have an admirable record of protecting the
human rights of minority groups. We have not, as a professional group,
participated in the deliberate murder of Jews just because they were Jews.
Nor are we likely to do so. Perhaps then, even though our professional
ethics may sometimes sanction questionable tactics, there really is no truly
significant lesson for the American lawyer to learn from the Holocaust.
Perhaps what he or she learned in high school or college, if anything, is
enough.

How you react to those thoughts depends in part on how you view
the Holocaust. You might, for example, consider the Holocaust to be the
ultimate demonstration of the peculiar vulnerability of Jews to injustice
and as the justification for Israel to take certain kinds of political action.
If you see the Holocaust as something having an impact on Jews only,
then perhaps there are no lessons in it for the American lawyer.

But if you view the Holocaust experience more broadly, as I do, then
there are lessons to be learned by American lawyers. We are far from per-
fect and, within our own code of ethics, there might be the beginnings of
disaster.

Is there any danger that American lawyers might become what
Franklin Littell has called "technically competent barbarians?"

What does Littell mean by "technically competent barbarians"? Germany had a system of law, a sophisticated system, which was interpreted
and applied by men trained in some of Europe's finest universities
(trained, by the way, before Hitler took over), learned men, men who

knew the law, men who were taught by their professors to be efficient and skillful. Those same men utilized their university-acquired knowledge and skills to murder millions of Jews and others. Those lawyers, who, in other facets of their lives, lived just as you and I, were among those Franklin Littell describes as technically competent barbarians.

As I have said, American lawyers have not participated in the killing of millions of people. It is, of course, true that that magnificent document, the United States Constitution, when first adopted, savaged an entire race of people—Blacks. Slavery was acknowledged and approved—for the sake of political expedience. Women were denied full participation in the process of government. Later, while the Nazis were killing Jews, we defined Americans of Japanese ancestry, living on the West Coast, as being in a special category and we interned them in camps in the California desert. We did not kill them, but we did deprive them of their liberty, their property and their right to pursue their vision of happiness.

But perhaps I go too far. Lawyers cannot be blamed for those things, at least not in the same way that German lawyers participated in the Holocaust. I think that's right. While I am uncomfortable with the fact that many—perhaps even most—lawyers were willing to support and participate in a legal system which consciously discriminated against many members of our society, that is not the same as killing those people. It is not the same, but it is also not nice. How close are American lawyers to becoming, under the philosophy of our code of ethics, "technically competent barbarians"?

In thinking about that, consider this: why was it wrong to kill the very first of the six million Jews? My answer is: that person had, by reason of his or her humanity, a right to continued life, free of interference from the state, even if the state thought that the common good would best be served by the killing of that person. The state had no moral authority to kill that Jew. That it had the legal power to do so is clear because it did kill.

Sometimes—or at least so it seems to me—professional rules foster professional barbarism, the same kind of professional barbarism that Franklin Littell complains about. For example, a lawyer may vigorously cross-examine a truthful, but emotionally fragile witness in an attempt to break him or her down, thus undermining the impact of the witness' unfavorable testimony.

Note what is happening. The lawyer, to protect his or her client, is permitted to attack the dignity and integrity of another human being. The lawyer will argue that our judicial system is one of the best and that occasional abuses must be tolerated in order to protect our method of resolving societal conflicts. That is a perfectly rational argument. My problem with it is this: It assumes that the common good (as the lawyer sees it) justifies the denial of what I see as one person's basic human right, the right of personal dignity.

From my perspective the human right of dignity of the witness cannot properly be sacrificed at the lawyer's altar anymore than the Black's freedom can be sacrificed at the white South African's economic altar or the Jew's life could be taken to satisfy the political theories of a once civilized society. If the American lawyer, wittingly or unwittingly, accepts the principle that human rights are subordinate to the personal preferences of those who control the instruments of power, then we are at risk: we could become technically competent barbarians.

Can the American lawyer believe in human rights and also believe that it is acceptable, professional behavior to inflict emotional damage on a truthful, adverse witness? I expect that the ordinary lawyer would answer: Of course I can believe in human rights and also believe in the appropriateness of vigorous cross-examination. My client has a right to have the State prove that he is guilty and my job is to make certain that the presumption of innocence is protected. I do that by forcing the state to prove its case, every time. My actions are in the best interest of all the people and if, from time to time, the emotional well-being of a person must be sacrificed, the great goal is worth it.

I think that most of us would agree that America's "presumption of innocence" is a worthwhile presumption. I also believe that most of us would agree that the State should not be permitted to deprive us of our liberty without first proving, beyond a reasonable doubt, that we are guilty of the charge, whatever the charge might be. Those things are not the question. The question is: should a lawyer be permitted to sacrifice the rights of one person (the witness) in order to protect another person (his client) from being punished by the State (which is, in the final analysis, all of us)?

If you view human rights as being rights which humans have, *except* that those rights are subordinate to the legitimate needs of society, i. e., the majority of those in power, then lawyers can say: Yes, I can believe in human rights and also believe in the correctness of destroying the witness in order to defend my client because in so doing I am acting for the good of society generally.

I confess that I view human rights differently. I view them as something inherent in every person without regard to the accidents of race, religion, sex or temporary situation, e. g., being a witness. Those inherent rights cannot legitimately be taken away from any one of us just because a majority of those in power believe it is best for the greatest number if we do so. Under my view, inalienable rights—human rights—are not to be sacrificed to serve the convenience of the majority—not in Germany and not in America.

I suggest that lawyers who really believe in human rights should contemplate the Holocaust, extract underlying general philosophical principles and reexamine the rationale which underlies the ethics of our adversary system.

Chapter VI Endnotes

1. Roger C. Crampton, "The Ordinary Religion of the Law School Classroom," 29 *Journal of Legal Education* (1978): 237ff.

2. Harold J. Berman, "The Interaction of Law and Religion," 8 *Capitol University Law Review* (1979): 345, 346.

3. *Ibid.*, p. 350.

Chapter VII

PRESERVING THE PERSONAL STORY: THE ROLE OF VIDEO DOCUMENTATION

Geoffrey H. Hartman

To bear witness involves two parties: those who testify, and those who are obligated to hear the testimony. For a time after the Holocaust, those who bore witness found only a few who could bear hearing about their experiences. The rest did not wish to hear, any more than when the events were happening. Haim Gouri, the poet and filmmaker, calls the second part of his trilogy *The Eighty-First Blow*. The title is taken from the case of a man punished in a camp and left for dead after eighty blows. When, as a survivor he tried to tell his story, he was not believed. That was the eighty-first blow, more killing than the others.

Interviews of survivors were first recorded by David Boder, a Professor of Psychology at the Illinois Institute of Technology. They were made in the summer of 1945 on an early version of our tape recorder, a magnetic wire machine just developed by the Armour Research Foundation. "Through the wire recorder," Dr. Boder wrote, "the displaced person could relate in his own language in his own voice the story of his concentration camp life."[1] That principle still guides, for example, the videotape project of the Yale Archive for Holocaust Testimonies. The survivors should tell their stories in their own language and in their own voice. Otherwise their humanity is alienated a second time; their very memories are taken from them.

It was, in fact, the television series *Holocaust* that prompted the New Haven chapter of the *Farband*, comprised mainly of survivors, to agree to form a "Holocaust Survivors Film Project." The influential medium of television was trivializing or falsifying their past, they felt. They would break a silence most of them had kept. Immediately after World War II their business had been to return to normalcy, and not to live in the past. Besides, few Americans had the strength to listen. But now, in 1979, with old age approaching, their numbers diminishing, their children grown up, their social standing secure, it was important to disclose what had been done and suffered. *Zachor*, the command to remember, could not be left to the media or even to the historians.

Every recording device is partial and defective. Questionnaires are coldly informative and rarely convey the feeling of the life actually lived. Audiotape does better, but the voice it transmits is strangely disembodied, and audio tape collections tend to become inert unless transcribed. Most of Boder's interviews, for example, are still not available. His book, published in 1949, contains eight selected conversations. Videotaped testimony, which adds body to voice, so that we *see* the witness reliving his memories, is the closest we will ever get to the person. It may strike some viewers as an invasion of the survivor's privacy. Yet each one has come forward of his or her own will. Besides, despite the immediacy of such recordings, they are powerful rather than appalling because their imagery is not static as in those grim black-and-white pictures that were circulated after the opening of the camps, and which still make up the main exhibit of many museums. However terrible the story of most survivors, the courage shown by them in undergoing the experience again, if only in the form of memory, comes through. This time the survivor is more than a victim, more than the living carcass to which the camps systematically reduced every inmate.

Even television, of course, produces its own sense of unreality. Since Vietnam, we have seen too much that is unbelievably cruel. Videotaped interviews, moreover, can degenerate into a talk-show format, with the host gushing over the survivor, how strong, heroic, wonderful such a person must be. The very intimacy of the medium is as much a danger as its graphic and sensational impact. Yet our testimonies counter both this sensationalism and this trivialization. The camera focuses on a living person whose story, however painful, is part of that person. These are not ghostly voices from the past, or macabre and animated images. The very words, the recollections (fallible or not), the specific points of crisis, the small revealing details which always emerge, validate themselves. It is amazing how each story strikes home as unique although the basic facts are always the same and well known. The humanity of such a record is in the telling of it, its tone and emphasis, the transitions, the images used. "My metaphors are my wounds," Nelly Sach wrote.

Many have suggested that after Auschwitz there can be no art. Yet art has always been under accusation for its inadequacy, its inability to represent the unbelievable event. Even the most realistic media accounts of the Holocaust seem hollow, or disqualify the mode of realism. Abstract or stylized representations are even more dubious: they create exploitative mixtures of horror and refinement. Yet the victims themselves did not repudiate art: many recorded on toilet paper, scraps, margins, whatever could be inscribed and smuggled out. Art or history, what did it matter to them? They heeded the injunction, "Thou shalt tell." Because of them we know the deadly facts, but also more than the deadly facts.

The distinction between history and self-expression collapsed in the face of an enemy bent on annihilating not only their individual but their collective existence, not only their physical presence but their memory—the very faculty that had distinguished and preserved them as a people. By testifying, the survivors, in effect, continue to deny victory to the powers of fabrication and forgetfulness that arise not only among those who still wish to silence them but also among those who honor them.

Alexander Donat tells us, in the name of the Warsaw historian Ignacy Schipper, that. . .

> everything depends on who transmits our testament to future generations, on who writes the history of this period. History is usually written by the victor....Should our murderers be victorious, should *they* write the history of this war, our destruction will be presented as one of the most beautiful pages of world history, and future generations will pay tribute to them as dauntless crusaders. Their every word will be taken for gospel. Or they may wipe out our memory altogether as if we had never existed, as if there had never been a Polish Jewry, a Ghetto in Warsaw, a Maidanek. Not even a dog will howl for us."[2]

By using the personal testimony, a form of expression with which all can identify, the survivors remind us that both history and art are based on the same kind of collective memory that sustained their ancestors.

After the mass murders perpetrated by the Nazi regime, a first duty, clearly, was to bring those who were responsible to justice. This also involved a massive inquest into the system of the camps, which was continued after the Nuremberg Trials by several organizations, including Yad Vashem, the National Museum and Archive in Israel that documented and verified every detail of a pattern which historian Raul Hilberg later arranged into an exact sequence: forced emigration, concentration (in ghettos and camps), extermination. Though pockets of ignorance remain, we have gained by now a highly specific map of the pattern of persecution, of every aspect of the systematic killing of six million Jews and millions of Russians, Poles, Armenians, Gypsies and others. The Yale Testimonies do not expect to add to this historical body of knowledge: they wish to focus on the individual rather than the mass, on each person's embodied and ongoing story, on the mind as it struggles with its memories, making sense of or simply facing them, on transmitting in oral form each version of survival.

When the camps were liberated, a group of involuntary witnesses was created and an unfinished film was made which some of you may have seen.[3] It records what the British Army found at Bergen-Belsen, in particular. It is a film that cannot be watched. Not because of its horror but because of its terrible monotony, as one after another naked body is picked up, carted off, thrown into the pit. This footage (rather than film) is a series of numb images: after seeing it, many may feel they cannot, or need not, see more. Yet it compels us to keep our eyes open. I was reminded of Anthony Burgess' *A Clockwork Orange*, in which a young punk is inoculated against crime by being kept awake to observe so much violence that he became nauseated.

Educationally, we do not believe in such forcible methods. This sort of involuntary witnessing shuts us down. Though we cannot forget, we also cannot develop those images. They may return to haunt us, they may even induce us to utter a vow that such an event must never occur again. But I suspect that one can endure this literal nakedness, this vulnerability and defilement, when conveyed by pictures which still assault us on entering most Holocaust museums. They create at best a feeling of rage and resolve, yet at worst a dangerous fascination with the very evil they portray, an identification with the aggressor. This is all the more so when they are juxtaposed with Riefenstahl's magnifications of the 1936 Olympics, overblown stills of the gigantic Nazi rallies and rituals—apocalyptic kitsch, as Saul Friedlander rightly calls it,[4] yet which arouses in us the old desire for an absolute purity or an all-absorbing discipline.

The Bergen-Belsen images, moreover, though filmed by the liberators, are not essentially different from those recorded by the killers themselves. Their context is liberation, but their content reflects, primarily, destruction and bondage. Fortunately, there are also moving sequences of the liberated survivors' joy, their rediscovery of human help and compassion, enfranchised bodies. It is one of our problems that few photo-documents survive which see the Holocaust from the side of the victims. I remember being asked by the curator of a memorial center which one—there was only *one*—of the many grim photos before us was by a survivor. It stood out: two people, perhaps husband and wife, touching each other through the barbed wire that separated them.

After we have learned the worst, after the exact numbers and dates have been etched into our minds, and the documents archived and preserved, then, especially, must we listen to the survivors themselves. Unfortunately, this is not a common practice: we often impose our own ordering categories, which enable us, or our children, to draw meaning out of experiences that forever threaten it. Words like "dignity," "martyrdom," "tragedy," even "spiritual resistance" are impotent—as Lawrence Langer has pointed out—to encompass what really happened.[5] They make use of language as a refuge; they allow some comfort, some belated grieving; but they should not deceive us by dignifying those innumerable death-masks and bodies which leave the viewer's mind in a state close to rigor mortis.

It is not only the big words but also the daily ones that become questionable. "We say, 'hunger,'" writes Primo Levi, author and survivor, "we say 'tiredness,' 'fear,' 'pain,' we say 'winter' and they are different things.

They are free words, created and used by free men who lived in comfort and suffering in their homes."[6] Of course, students of this period know only too well the euphemistic evasions of the perpetrators: "Resettlement," "Special Treatment," "Cleansing," "Final Solution." Hannah Arendt has given a frightening portrayal of Eichmann's mode of speech, full of what she calls "elating clichés."[7] But there is also the euphemistic language of the victims, which is justified in them, though not in us, and which Primo Levi, again, points to with ferocious bitterness when he writes: "Do you know how one says 'never' in camp slang? '*Morgen Furen*,' tomorrow morning." For many the sun would not rise, so fragile had the passage of time become.

To give up such euphemisms is almost impossible, because the only way to integrate the trauma of the death camps is by extending the prayers and rituals of the victim's own community — by Days of Remembrance, for example — that collectivize the event and make it ceremonious. David Roskies has recently written an historical account of the Jewish people's responses to catastrophe, and how they adapted songs and prayers in sacred or even satirical fashion.[8] Sometimes this adaptation occurs at a less deliberate yet equally significant level. A survivor recalls that, as a baby, he was secretly transferred from his mother to a foster mother, swaddled in a special blanket. He knows he was too young to remember the event, but this is the story handed down even as he was handed on — and as, in the Jewish tradition, Moses himself was saved.

This assimilative and often sanctifying perspective is better than remaining silent, or having ordinary words reveal such referential incompetence that language becomes totally duplicitous. In one Yale testimony, the survivor swears that Auschwitz had no dawn, that the sun that rose was black, and the moon was not the moon. Understanding, in those conditions, forces us to reflect on how ordinary words stabilize the world by anesthetizing us. Saul Friedlander can make a shocking comparison between the Revisionists, who deny the existence of the death camps, and honest historical research. "Revisionism," he writes, "purifies the past by trafficking in facts. At the opposite extreme, systematic historical research, which uncovers the facts in their most precise and most meticulous inter-connection, also protects us from the past, thanks to the inevitable paralysis of language. This is the exorcism and *the involuntary evasion to which we are all subject.*"[9]

We therefore have an obligation to hear out what each survivor has to say — even if, and perhaps because, their autonomy as human beings was jeopardized by the most brutal and systematic deculturation ever devised. Now that the state of gathering information for writing the history of the Holocaust is considerably advanced, a further task emerges. We must refuse to intellectualize prematurely, or generalize about the mentality of either survivor or aggressor. Perhaps we can apply a lesson from a philosophical controversy of the Middle Ages and say, God knows these things only in their particularity, never in their generality. Research should go on, must go on; but let us beware of creating a false science that tries to master this event by a professional deformation that flatters our competence as historians or psychologists, at the price of excluding the nearness and pathos of these individual stories.

Only these testimonies, heard out, and then compared, may yield the outlines of a way of thinking and talking that will not profane what happened. And if it were not intellectually obligatory, we would still need those voices and stories, and especially on film, because what we presently have is mainly the mocking and gloating photos of the aggressors.

We come now to a last and most difficult issue. How does one interview survivors? How can we assure them their own story, that is, exclude the interviewer's preconceptions and — above all — free up memories?

I have no good answers, and I doubt very much that a particular methodology will guarantee success in this area. In Holland, Dr. Bastiaans has resorted to LSD to induce a controlled regression that would break the survivors' silence or psychic immobility. In some, however, the blocking agent has taken the form of fluency — of doctrinaire or reconstructed versions of what occurred.

The interviewers, too, have their problems. One common preconception is that every survivor is febrile, and that activating a survivor's memories may also activate trauma. The interviewer may try to keep the witness from reliving his past too intensely. Hence, an unconscious distancing, a refusal to come too close. In one session this was even physically obvious because the interviewer allowed the survivor to read a long statement instead of talking spontaneously, to sit behind a table that separated her from the interviewer, and to mask herself with tinted glasses. Such distancing is often encouraged by those who over-identify with the witness — nonsurvivor interviewers, for example, who may harbor guilt about America's inaction during the war, or children of survivors who may be fearful of hurting the older generation. In fact, we have found that the witnesses who volunteer are tough and resilient, even though after testifying they may suffer from the return of memory. That is one reason why, in such cases, the taping is done only after a pre-interview and with the help of a support group that contains a psychologist or a mental health professional.

The most sensitive issue in interviewing is when to intervene, that is, interrupt a survivor's narration. At Yale we try to gain as free-flowing a testimony as possible. Yet interviewers should not fade out entirely, or pretend they are not present. They remain potential dialogue-partners, who have internalized crucial questions. What is told should not be told just to the cameras. As Dori Laub of Yale expressed it, the interviewer is a companion on this journey and must occasionally risk intruding. The psychoanalytical dialogue is a model here, when tactfully conducted; yet every physician I have talked with says that tact is related to timing and cannot be methodized.

It is difficult to filter out entirely the preoccupations of the inter-viewer, especially in this charged situation. Moreover, each taping session is bound to be affected by what may have happened on the day or week before and by the overall purpose of the project. We will eventually have some follow-up taping; yet it is hard to question survivors a second time. We are not undertaking interrogations. Yet eventually we hope to or-ganize an in-depth study of some of the people who have given their tes-timonies.

The overall aim of the project is educational. What this once meant, in terms of interviewing, is that we sometimes pretended to know less, and put ourselves in the place of a younger audience. From the point of view of the researcher, therefore, some of these questions may appear naive. Looking back at our early interviews, which were made in makeshift surroundings and with a minimum of help, I now think adopt-ing a naive persona did not really contribute very much. It is better to allow the teachers to explain and develop whatever seems unclear, since the interviews are not meant to be shown cold, but always with a teacher or a survivor present to enter into a dialogue with the young people in high school or college, for whom these interviews were made.

The questions we ask—or do not ask but wait to hear answered—con-cern the day-to-day, night-to-night existence, the human and psychological milieu: how it felt then, how it feels now. These testimonies are texts, not because we wish to study them as literature—that would be another way of profaning them—but because they are unintegrated, exposed, fal-lible memories that need interpretation. From the four hundred personal testimonies already deposited, and the two hundred we still hope to gather, an oral history is emerging that refuses to neglect feeling in order to focus on fact, and which does not seek the exceptional story but a pic-ture of "the rank and file experience" [Boder], the everyday life and death. But video-testimonies should not be used, either, to substitute emotion for thought, or tears for the scholar's resolute and continuous inquiry into the character of the perpetrators, their methods, the nature of the system or other issues of conscience that recur as long as "experts of the cheap word" [Erik Erikson on Hitler] inflame prejudice and gain power by set-ting one man's hand against the other.

The Yale testimonies, and others like them being made throughout the country—while the survivors are yet alive—will make it harder for even the most conscientious of us to seek refuge in an explanatory theory of redemptive message instead of staying with the words and feelings of those directly involved.

Chapter VII Endnotes

1. David P. Boder, *I Did Not Interview The Dead* (Urbana: The University of Illinois Press, 1949).

2. Alexander Donat, *The Holocaust Kingdom* (New York: Holt, Rinehart and Winston, 1965). See also Alvin H. Rosenfeld, *A Double Dying: Reflections on Holocaust Literature* (Bloomington and London: Indiana University Press, 1980), chapter 2. (For both books, use ADL order form in this issue — Ed.)

3. No title. Footage stored in The Imperial War Museum of Great Britain.

4. Saul Friedlander, *Reflections on Nazism: An Essay on Kitsch and Death* (New York: Harper and Row, 1982).

5. Lawrence L. Langer, *Versions of Survival: The Holocaust and the Human Spirit* (Albany: State University of New York, 1982).

6. Primo Levi, *Survival in Auschwitz*, trans. Stuart Woolf (New York: Collier, 1961). (Use ADL order form in this issue — Ed.)

7. Hannah Arendt, *Eichmann in Jerusalem: A Report on the Banality of Evil* (Rev. and enlarged ed. New York: Viking Press, 1965). See especially Chapter 3 and "Postscript." Also, Nachman Blumenthal, "On the Nazi Vocabulary," in *Yad Vashem Studies* I (Jerusalem: Jerusalem Post Press, 1957).

8. David P. Roskies, *Against The Apocalypse: Responses to Catastrophe in Modern Jewish Culture* (Cambridge, Mass.: Harvard University Press, 1984).

9. Friedlander.

Chapter VIII

THE HOLOCAUST SURVIVOR: SHIFTING IMAGES IN AMERICAN LITERATURE

Alan L. Berger

The Holocaust, notes Yosef Yerushalmi, has "already engendered more historical research than any single event in Jewish History." But, he hastens to add, the *Shoah*'s image "is being shaped, not at the historian's anvil, but in the novelist's crucible." Yerushalmi's unexpected observation directs our attention to literary encounters with the Holocaust and to the changing images of survivors which appear in such fiction. Three approaches to survivors have emerged in American Jewish fiction. In chronological order they are fear, mystery and awe, and, most disturbing, exploitation. Survivors have, in some instances, gone from victims to vengeance seekers. How can these changes be accounted for and what are their possible meanings?

At the outset it is crucial to note that both the concept of surviving and the notion of literary authenticity require rethinking after Auschwitz. Much has been written concerning the many paradoxes endangered by the Holocaust. But there is no greater paradox than the disbelief which greeted the victims' accounts of their experience. Survivors found that their stories were literally unbelievable. The conceptual underpinnings of this cruel paradox have been well described by Hannah Arendt, who observed that the enormity of their crimes guaranteed that the Nazis, who protested their innocence with all manner of lies, would be more believed than the victims who told the truth. The unbelievability of Holocaust horror affected even the Jews. For example, Elie Wiesel's *Night* tells of the communal rebuff which greeted Moché the Beadle's attempt to warn Sighet's Jews of their impending doom.

Non-witnesses, both Jews and Christians, were influenced by pictures of liberated camps with mounds of corpses and the stick-like survivors who walked among them, the living barely distinguishable from the dead. What was one to do with survivors whose very existence challenged

Western cultural assumptions about the nature of death and the value of life? Society could deal with martyrs and heroes but could not cope with survivors who were evidently neither martyrs nor heroes. Henry Krystal and William Niederland write that survivors of disasters and persecutions "are suspected of unfair play, collaboration with the enemy, or harlotry. On a deeper psychological level, there is a fear of survivors akin to the fear of a returning ghost."

Holocaust literature written by non-witnessing authors represents an enormously complex issue. On the one hand, there is the necessity to learn from and bear witness to the *Shoah*. Yet, with the passage of time, there occur distortions, falsifications, de-Judaizing of the catastrophe, and even the obscenity of denials that the Holocaust occurred. The tendency to de-Judaize the Holocaust in America began with the controversy over the Broadway production of Anne Frank's Diary (1955). Arguing against Meyer Levin's version on the grounds that it was "too Jewish" for Gentile audiences, Lillian Hellman succeeded in having a play presented which falsely universalized Anne's words. This contemporary expression of banalizing or domesticating the Holocaust prompted Levin to ask "What gave the playwrights the right to change Anne's profound words about Jewish particularism [to] the wishy-washy generalization about human suffering?" Levin's observation underlines the unfortunate tendency of many to subsume the Holocaust under the cliché of "man's inhumanity to man," thereby missing the epoch-making nature of the Event. His own Holocaust novel *Eva* (1959) was written from an unmistakably Jewish and Zionist point of view. After making a harrowing escape from Auschwitz, Eva flees to Israel where she marries and raises a family.

Serious students of Holocaust literature have noted the presence of a dialectical tension between speech and silence. The same type of dialectic is at work in literary treatments of survivors. On the one hand, Wiesel notes that the Holocaust has transformed some writers "into more genuinely intense artists."   Although they are few, certain thinkers, educators, and novelists are having a real impact, proving "that even those who have not experienced the event may learn to be worthy of it." The Holocaust fiction of Hugh Nissenson and Cynthia Ozick demonstrates the accuracy of Wiesel's contention. But Wiesel has also observed that "between the dead and the rest of us there exists an abyss that no talent can comprehend."

The third type of approach to survivors — exploitation of faddishness — was anticipated early by Wiesel who felt compelled to rescue the survivors a second time, not from the Nazis, but from contemporary pseudo-intellectuals and know-nothing theorists. "A Plea for the Dead" (1967) warns that those who blame the Jews for their own deaths blaspheme against the victims. "The dead," writes Wiesel, "have earned something better than this posthumous humiliation." "A Plea for the Survivors" (1977) speaks of contemporary societies' exploitation, distortion, monopolization, embellishment, and debasement of survivors' suffering, according to the needs of the moment.

Historical Examples: Fear of Survivors

Edward Lewis Wallant's *The Pawnbroker* (1961) portrays the pre-Holocaust world, the Holocaust experiences, and the post-Holocaust existence of Sol Nazerman, who prior to the war had been a European professor of intellectual history. Nazerman lost his family, his confidence in the nobility of ideas, and his Jewish convictions in the *Shoah*'s flames. In America, Sol operates an East Harlem pawnshop for a criminal partner, is plagued by holocaustal memories which intensify each August at the time of his murdered family's *yahrzeit*, and rejects those around him.

The novel's plot centers on the relationship between Sol and his Puerto Rican assistant, Jesus Ortiz, to whom Sol is both teacher and mentor. Conspirator in a failed robbery attempt, Jesus in fact dies for Sol by stepping in front of the pawnbroker as a fatal shot is fired. Sol, who throughout the story had sought only solitude — "I am safe within myself" — begins to weep at Jesus' murder, and turns toward those whom he had earlier rejected.

Sol Nazerman's novelistic appearance denoted a new figure in American literature — "concentration camp man." Physically deformed as a result of Nazi torture, Sol wishes to puncture even the smallest dreams with his ugliness. He is dirty as opposed to the novel's social worker, Marilyn Birchfield, whose New England cleanliness would only be defiled by contact with Sol. The survivor even declares that Marilyn should not love him, as she would then be guilty of necrophilia.

Wallant's treatment of survivors is, however, ambivalent. On the one hand, he succeeds in portraying the variety of post-Holocaust faith orientations among these people. Sol is an atheist who thinks God is cruel. "Kill us," Sol says, but admonishes the divine to do so only once. The pawnbroker's pre-war Jewish fidelity is forever shattered. Tessie, his mistress, is a secularist whose death camp experiences have left her with the desire to scream all day. Nonetheless, she lights *yahrzeit* candles for her dead family and friends. Mendel is Tessie's aged father who suffered horribly in the camps but remained a faithfully religious Jew who, on his death bed, utters the prayer *Sh'ma Yisrael*.

But, the image of the survivor in *The Pawnbroker* is one of a physically damaged, psychically scarred individual who is apologetic for having survived and who distills no lessons, either societal or specifically Jewish, from his experience. Suffering is the novel's major theme, but Wallant suggests a continuum of human misery ranging from the death camps to the suburbs. "Life," wrote Wallant, "is man under a sentence of death." Wallant's survivor reflects the initial stage in society's approach to the *Shoah*.   Wallant ends, however inadvertently, by trivializing the

Holocaust, thereby ignoring the survivor's pedagogical role and denying the audience access to warning signs in their own culture.

Mystery and Awe

The decade of the sixties also marked a new beginning of societal awareness of the Holocaust. Increasing research on what had happened in Europe, the effect of the internationally televised Eichmann trial, the writings of Wiesel and other survivor novelists, and realization on the part of clinical psychiatrists that survivors' traumas could be mirrored in the lives of their children all coalesced to form the matrix out of which emerged Holocaust fiction whose authors recognized the *Shoah* was, in the words of Irving Greenberg, "an orienting event."

Hugh Nissenson's 1963 short story "The Law" is, in contrast to *The Pawnbroker*, a model of the post-Holocaust Jewish covenantal quandary. Willi Levy, a pre-war assimilationist German Jew, had survived Bergen-Belsen, come to America, married a refugee, and become the father of Daniel. The story concerns Willi's Holocaust testimony told with ritual intensity to Daniel as the latter prepared for his bar-mitzvah. The son's *haftarah* portion deals with some of the law. Nissenson indicts Christian complicity in the Holocaust in the person of an SS man at Bergen-Belsen. Scion of a family of pastors, the murderer knew the Decalogue by heart, unlike Willi. Willi is uncertain of the *Shoah*'s meaning but affirms, through his son's bar-mitzvah, that the Law must be passed from father to son as Jews have traditionally done.

"The Law" enumerates features of survivors which were to be elaborated in the decade of the seventies. Nissenson recognizes, for example, that the *Shoah* may, in fact, have a positive aspect to its legacy. Willi is neither a societal embarrassment nor a saint. His is the first example known to me of a survivor portrayed as a parent. Daniel is, therefore, the earliest literary child of survivors. Although not sketched in detail, the son's presence is a harbinger of the second generation phenomenon. Unlike Wallant, Nissenson's survivor has adopted a Jewishly particularistic orientation. His attempt to reconstruct a moral universe leads to his insistence that Daniel become a bar-mitzvah. He rejects Jewish-Christian dialogue and is determined to tell his Holocaust tales, although realizing that non-witnesses can never fully understand the camps. Willi's post-Holocaust turn to Judaism is a literary expression of Emil Fackenheim's notion that Jewish endurance is itself a mystery in the religious sense of the term. Nisserson's tale underscores the complexity of the post-Holocaust divine-human relationship.

Norma Rosen's *Touching Evil* (1969) boldly attempts to universalize the Holocaust's message. Dealing with the effect of the Eichmann trial on two American Christian women, one of whom is pregnant, the novel seeks to confront radical evil and the altered perception of humanity which an awareness of what humans are capable of doing to one another

yields. Rosen's novel rightly contends that Holocaust testimony is trans-
formative, and that both men and God are implicated in the *Shoah*. Far
from Wallant's understanding, Rosen's main character Jean Lamb contends that there are two kinds of people: those who know about the
Holocaust and those who do not. And, she adds, knowing about the
Holocaust has nothing to do with reading the newspaper. Moreover, the
mounds of corpses and destroyed humanity will, Jean Lamb is convinced,
became — much in the manner of Stonehenge and Angkor Wat — civiliza-
tional icons, a metaphysical landmark of the twentieth century. *Touching
Evil* is a conceptually daring novel which attempts to sensitize non-Jews to
holocaustal trauma. Yet, there are no flesh and blood survivors interact-
ing with Christians. Survivors are distanced both geographically (they are
six thousand miles away in Israel) and through the medium of television.
Rosen's work can, nevertheless, be seen as a transitional novel in its stress
on the Holocaust's widening circle of victims.

The decade of the seventies heralded the appearance of Holocaust
novels by Jewishly secure Jewish American writers displaying a new sensitivity toward survivors. *Mr. Sammler's Planet* (1970) and *Anya* (1974) are
two pioneer novels showing survivors in their multifaceted complexity.
Moving considerably beyond Wallet's apologia and penetrating Rosen's
use of distance, these works portray survivors' moral insight and salvific
wisdom. In Sammler's case, there is considerable interaction with both
Jews and society at large, whereas Anya lives among and interacts only
with Jews in her post-*Shoah* existence. Survivors are links with a murdered people, but they also underscore the fragility of the Jewish condition in America. Their message to American Jewry seems, on one level,
to be a reminder of Jewish specificity or, in Fackenheim's telling phrase,
"the condition of being singled out." Reflecting careful historical research
and, in the case of *Anya*, extensive interviews with a survivor, these novels
not only provide a wealth of information concerning survivors' pre-war
lives, but also give accounts of the various ways in which Jews were caught
in the Nazi Kingdom of Death.

Psychologically, survivors now were seen as participants in what
Robert Jay Lifton terms a struggle for meaning. This struggle or "survivor
mission" helped focus attention on survivors' hopes for the future as well
as their relationship to the past. In the cases of Arthur Sammler and
Anya Savikin, such missions involved a preservation of Jewish traditional,
although not religious, values, and a specific relationship to their
daughters, both of whom were survivors. While Sammler and Anya are in-
describably different from their American Jewish acquaintances, and
while both are physically exceptional, both are described as being concerned with the Jewish and human future. Their Holocaust legacies, like
Willi Levy's, manifest positive elements. Anya's is specifically Jewish.
She goes to extraordinary lengths to insure that her daughter marry en-
dogamously, not just an American Jew, but an Israeli. Sammler's legacy is
universal. An intellectual, he fights against the apocalyptic nihilism which

he finds so prevalent both in American culture and among certain of his survivor friends.

Survivors during this decade were also portrayed as mystics whose tales could transform even their less Jewishly sensitive American listeners. Cynthia Ozick, who launched the decade of the seventies with a programmatic essay outlining the need for liturgical literature (by which she meant a specifically Jewish as opposed to American type of writing), provides a case in point. In her early Holocaust novels *Bloodshed* (1976) and "Levitation" (1982), survivors are the only authentic Jews. *Bloodshed's* survivor figure is a rebbe (hasidic mystic) who, like Sol Nazerman, had been victimized by a Nazi medical experiment. Unlike Sol, however, the rebbe's Holocaust experience made him a "believer in turnings form folly, error, and a mistaken life." In the post-Holocaust world the rebbe probes deeper [into] and wrestles more profoundly [than ever before] with issues of faith and skepticism. He accomplishes this task, however, within the context of a newly formed hasidic community located outside of New York City and intended by Ozick to indicate the covenant antagonism of much of American culture. "Levitation" combines the figure of refuge and survivor in the person of an anonymous guest at a party. The outsider's theological anguish is both inconsolable and compelling to his listeners. The man remembers the Holocaust as a time when "the eyes of God were shut. Shut...like iron doors." The mysterious messenger can only express his pain by telling tales of the *Shoah*. Transformed by his Holocaust tales, the room itself levitates and "all the Jews are in the air."

Arthur A. Cohen's *In the Days of Simon Stern* (1973) utilizes messianic and mythic themes to tell the tale of a contemporary Jewish messiah whose self-appointed task is to rescue a Jewish remnant from the camps. Nathan the scribe, blinded in the death camps, plays a crucial role in the novel. Although physically blind, he is a seer with exceptionally keen vision. In fact, Simon Stern, Cohen's literary messiah, contends that all must learn to see as does Nathan. Like Artur Sammler, Nathan's seeing is salvific. The novel maintains that survivors, as embodied in the figure of Nathan, possess penitential patience and are able to recognize the profound intricacies which characterize the post-Auschwitz relationship between man and God, and the profound theodical issues raised by the death camps.

Stefan Kanfer's *The Eighth Sin* (1978) is a remarkable novel written by a Jewish non-witness. It concerns the post-Holocaust existence of a Gypsy survivor, Benoit Kaufman. Ben is a teenager at war's end when airlifted to England where he remains silent for three months in reaction to the unspeakable horrors he has witnessed. An orphan and an artist, Ben is adopted by a Jewish couple. He accompanies them to New York, gets in trouble with the law, becomes a successful commercial artist, marries, is divorced, tracks down and murders a fellow Gypsy, Eleazar Jassy, who collaborated with the Nazis and is his brother. At novel's end Ben returns to Europe where he is a solitary wanderer.

The eighth, and deadliest, sin is forgetting. "Memory," contends Ben, "stained the present like a testimonial curse." The novel deftly inter-weaves Benoit's tale with historical documentation and testimony concerning the fate of Europe's Gypsies. Kanfer also exposes post-Holocaust prejudices against Gypsies. Ben penetrates the euphemisms of contemporary language. Instead of murder, for example, he prefers the Gypsy term *Morteur*. At least, he thinks, it contains death. The Gypsy's anger at linguistic deceit is most intense when he thinks of the word Holocaust, "a nothing category; a eunuch of a word." It only has significance to the Jews. "To the rest of this numb world it means fire. To the Gypsies, even less."

Kanfer wisely links Gypsies and Jews. On the airplane ferrying or-phaned children to London, Ben repeats the *Sh'ma Yisrael* prayer uttered by his Jewish companion. Victimization and sensitivity to holocaustal pain and suffering unite Gypsy and Jew. Ben can, for example, contend that the Holocaust is "the shit of civilization." But he, like Wiesel, knows that "this was a subject that could kill you if you let it." Casting the Gypsy survivor as a portrait painter, Kanfer shows his readers that survivors can see through camouflage and disguise. For example, daily radio reports contend that Nazis are being rehabilitated. No punishment is to be meted out for those who Telford Taylor termed the "running dogs of murder."

Despite this kinship of suffering, a vast difference exists between Jewish and Gypsy literary reaction to the Holocaust. The Jewish survivor, in the decade of the seventies, strives for meaning by seeking to teach holocaustal lessons. For Benoit, on the other hand, it is vengeance rather than pedagogy or testimony which proves irresistible. Although both act on behalf of the dead, Benoit builds nothing and has nothing. On the other hand, Wisel's Elisha in *Dawn* is morally torn by his act of murder committed in the act of building the Jewish state. *The Eighth Sin* is, however, an important Holocaust novel in its focus on the survivor of a group about whom too little is known.

Exploitation: Survivor As Fad

William Styron's *Sophie's Choice* (1979) illustrates the perils of anti-historical approaches to the Holocaust and revisionist denials of Nazi evil. Ostensibly a novel of the *Shoah*, the book is really concerned with sex, the lingering antagonisms of the Civil War, and—one suspects—the author's attempt to prove that he can write a better Holocaust novel than any Jewish writer. The plot focuses on the troubled postwar life of Sophie Zawistowska, a Polish non-Jew who, upon her arrival in Auschwitz, was forced to choose which of her two children would be sent immediately to the gas chamber. In Brooklyn, her life and destiny are inextricably bound to Nathan Landau, a brilliant but psychotic Jew, whose actions indict what Styron perceives as Jewish indifference to the Holocaust suffering of non-Jewish victims. This incredible feat is accomplished by having Nathan ver-

bally and physically torment Sophie. Stingo, a young Southern writer—
Styron himself at the beginning of his career—travels to this "kingdom of
the Jews" in order to work on the great American novel. At story's end,
Sophie and Nathan have committed suicide. Stingo, reacting to this news,
travels to Coney Island where, after sleeping all night on the beach, he
awakes and thinks, "Morning: excellent and fair."

Focusing on just one of the many problems raised by Styron's work,
let us enquire about the dangers of false universalization. There is an ongoing debate concerning the relationship between particular and universal
lessons of the Holocaust. While it is true that there were many other victims of Nazism, the Holocaust was specifically intended to rid Europe of
its Jews. Cynthia Ozick has wisely observed of Auschwitz that, "like any
successful factory in roaring production, the German death-factory
produced useful by-products: elimination of numbers of Slavs and most
Gypsies." Styron, for his part, appears blind to evil's particularity. He
describes Joseph Mengele, the infamous death doctor, as either "a
religious person," or "a failed believer seeking for redemption, groping for
faith." This moral obtuseness and historical ignorance is awesomely
depressing. But Styron is unable even to name the death doctor. Mengele is called Dr. Jemand von Niemand ("everyone from nobody"). Echo-
ing Hannah Arendt's view of evil's banality, Styron implies that nobody
was responsible for Auschwitz. This was the defense claim at the Nuremberg Trials in 1946, and those of the Auschwitz guards in Frankfort in
1964.

Styron's novel victimizes the victims a second time by robbing the
Jews of their deaths. Commenting on the contemporary lack of attention
to specificity, Wiesel observes "whosoever contributes to oblivion finishes
the killer's work." Styron, as noted, has the Polish Catholic Sophie die at
the hands of a Jew rather than a Nazi. Aside from outright revisionist
denials could there be more blatant denial of, or indifference to,
Holocaust history? Styron's novel is, in effect, a contemporary version of
the ancient *adversus Judaeos* tradition. Perhaps the most telling sign of
Styron's failure to grasp the radical evil of the Holocaust comes at the end
of the novel when Stingo, refreshed from his sleep, feels wonderful about
the future; a feeling emphasized in even greater detail in the film. One
should never feel good about the Holocaust. Stingo's good feeling can
only be based on forgetting, whereas writers of high seriousness who confront the *Shoah* speak constantly of remembering.

Midway through the decade of the eighties, and forty years after the
Shoah, the image of survivors in literature appears again to be changing.
There now seems to be a tendency to reduce survivors to the status of objects worthy of study, rather than viewing them as human beings who have
a salvific message for society. Ozick's short story "Rosa" (1983), for example, portrays the psychic distress of a survivor ignored by society and
pursued by a clinical psychologist who wishes her to take part in an
academic study he is conducting. The professor knows nothing of the

Holocaust and thinks that the passivity before death displayed by *Mussellmäner* is comparable to the Buddhist goal of non-attachment to things. Rosa knows that psychological attempts to explain away Auschwitz are doomed to failure. The cycle appears complete. Society's ignorance about and fear of survivors is replaced by a stage of fiction which celebrates their moral and potentially salvific powers. Ozick's latest fiction warns, however, that sensitivity has deteriorated into exploitation.

Ozick's novel, *The Cannibal Galaxy* (1983), describes an even more extreme situation. A survivor, Joseph Brill, has difficulty remembering the lessons of the *Shoah*. The novel's main character is not a survivor, but a refugee — Hester Lilt — who left Europe on a children's transport. It is she who provides a model of authentic Jewish reaction to catastrophe by clinging tenaciously to covenantal Judaism in response to historical disaster. This may be Ozick's way of contending that, as survivors disappear from among our ranks, it is up to the rest of us to learn the history and tell the story of the Holocaust.

Another development in the literary treatment of survivors has been the emergence of a new type of Holocaust novel written by children of survivors or specifically about them. The three I have in mind are Robert Greenfield's *Temple* (1982), Thomas Friedmann's *Damaged Goods* (1984), and Wiesel's *The Fifth Son* (1985). All three occur against the turbulent background of late nineteen-sixties America, and each focuses on college students as children or grandchildren of survivors. Unlike Nissenson's child of a survivor, the characters in these stories assume much fuller literary proportion. Greenfield's novel treats a boy whose grandfather is a survivor. The grandson feels that his generation, rather than his parents', is more sensitive to the survivors of the *Shoah*. This stance implies two things. It is, first of all, a literary expression of Hanson's sociological law: the third generation remembers what the second generation wants to forget. Second, Greenfield suggests that the survivors' message is being heard. There are, however, problems with this approach. Although the grandson feels for his survivor grandfather, he nonetheless distances the older man. The narrative, for example, alternates between first and third person. The grandson cannot cope with the older man's experiences.

Friedmann's autobiographic novel is more plausible in telling the story of the son of two Hungarian Jews who survived the Holocaust. Friedmann has an insider's eye for the detail and ritual of Orthodox Jewish life in America. His portrayal of the complex relationship between survivors and their children should, moreover, serve to dispel the sterotypical Jewish mother and father images so dear to satirists such as Philip Roth. A mother who is compassionate, and speaks of her Holocaust past, but disappears midway through the novel, and a stern father who never tells Holocaust tales both leave their indelible imprint upon their identity-seeking son. Both *Temple* and *Damaged Goods* testify to the continuity of Jewish tradition and to the fact that survivors, despite their Holocaust experiences, raised their children Jewishly.

Wiesel's latest exploration of the *Shoah* marks a radical departure in setting from his earlier works. *The Fifth Son* concerns an American-born child of survivors who, enveloped by his parent's past, seeks both his own identity and the meaning of post-Holocaust Jewish destiny. Set in the ritual context of Passover, the novel challenges post-Holocaust American Jews to confront the monumental covenantal challenges wrought by the Holocaust. The son, who assumes the name of his dead brother, seeks to complete his father's mission of vengeance against a Nazi who has murdered his parents' first son, Ariel. Wiesel reflects on the curious relationship between victim and victimizer. "I am tracking him down," observes the son, "and yet I am his prisoner." For such is the life of the survivor.

The Fifth Son portrays both the strengths and the obsessions of survivors. After the war, still unwanted by the world, survivors came to new countries, learned new languages and new vocational skills, and raised new families. Reuven Tamiroff, the father of both Ariels, composes letters to the dead Ariel in which he tells his murdered son of the recurring feeling of being "superfluous."

> No country will have us. No visas. Draconian quota restrictions. Debasing medical examinations. We are treated as slaves or beasts of burden.

The novel's central preoccupation is with the question of justice and guilt, and the sanctity of life. Reuven and Simha the Dark, a friend from the Ghetto, spend long hours discussing the issue of justifiable murder. Beginning with Moses' slaying of the Egyptian overseer, the two friends seek biblical and talmudic guidelines in attempting to reconcile their guilt feelings for having participated in the post-war assassination of Richard Lander, the so-called Angel of Ghetto Davarowsk.

Reuven's son, with the aid of his girlfriend, discovers that the Angel is still alive and about to receive an award for his philanthropic activities. Ariel travels to post-war Germany in order to confront the killer in his own city of Reshastaadt (evil city). The meeting between the two symbolizes the ongoing battle between good and evil. The American Ariel does not kill the Nazi, however, but instead pronounces a curse upon him for the crime of having "killed eternity in man."

Survivors in *The Fifth Son* refuse despair. They tell tales, have children, which in the post-Auschwitz age is itself an act fraught with messianic implications, and celebrate life — *Kiddush Ha-hayyim*. What remains uncertain is whether the second generation which came of age in the 1960s will be able to bear the covenantal burden imposed by the Holocaust past while (simultaneously) striving to ensure a Jewish future, which, for Wiesel, will be forever haunted by the past.

Conclusion:

Images of survivors in the fiction we have examined raise a host of questions. Does the world want to remember? The evidence is ambiguous. Anya recalls telling an American woman about the murder of her husband Stajoe. Finishing her tale, Anya is asked by her listener, "and how is Stajoe?" Why has the event been avoided by most serious Christian writers? Does this avoidance stem from a sense of shame or guilt? Is it attributable to the silence one embraces while standing before the horror in its awesomeness? Novels representing the persecuted, Jews and Gypsies, have attempted to enter this forbidden domain. Authentic portrayals of survivors are concerned about the meaning of suffering and the preciousness of endurance, expose both Christian and secularist hatred of minorities, and stress the importance of remembering. Serious Holocaust novels compel the reader to ponder the relationships among Israel, the Holocaust, non-Jews, and the common human future.

This brief survey suggests three broad conclusions. Novelists have a special pedagogical role to play in teaching about the Holocaust and its survivors. But the novelist as pedagogue is faced with special problems. It is one thing to emphasize the survivor as a link with the past and as a reminder of the necessity of remembering. But it is quite another matter to state that nearly 75 percent of the current world population was born after the second World War. For these multitudes it is not a question of memory, it is a matter of learning.

Second, it is important to emphasize that the *Shoah* has universal lessons to teach. Survivors have an elusive but ineluctable truth to tell the rest of us concerning the human condition. But to learn this truth it is imperative to recognize that old, pre-Holocaust categories have been destroyed by the *Shoah*. What, for example, is heroic, and who is a hero? Attempts to restrict our understanding of the *Shoah*, or to domesticate it in any way, are first on the road to forgetfulness. There is as well the paradox of hearing the survivors' testimony. Is this testimony already too late?

Finally, it is necessary to recognize the truth Wiesel has asserted concerning survivors: they are not and cannot be like us. If, however, we are wise enough, brave enough, and humble enough, we will listen to their stories and learn from them about the meaning of being human in an age of inhumanity. This is the true task of post-Holocaust literary pedagogy.

Chapter IX

LOOKING BACK: THE AMERICAN PROTESTANT CHURCHES IN 1945 AND WORLD WAR II

Robert W. Ross

The perspective of this paper is that of the American Protestant religious press in 1945, as the war in Europe came to an end. It seeks the response of the American Protestant Christian Churches to the developing events of 1945, as reflected in or reported by that press. The sources consulted were those periodicals used originally in preparation of *So It Was True, The American Protestant Press and the Nazi Persecution of the Jews*, for the year 1945. All of the periodicals for that year were reexamined without reference to the book.

At the outset it may be stated that seven major or central themes became evident during this reexamination. They are: 1) the strong, even urgent, desire to reestablish contact with the churches of formerly occupied Europe, including Germany, as quickly as possible; 2) the confrontation with the forced labor and concentration system through liberation of the still existing concentration camps; 3) the whole question of the use of the Atomic Bomb in Japan; 4) the commitment of the highest quality churchmen and resources to the task of reestablishing and rehabilitating Europe's churches; 5) astonishment and dismay at the extent of the war damage, particularly to churches, and at the immensity of the refugee problem including need for food, clothing, housing, medical supplies, blankets and, above all else, the spector of starvation; 6) the emerging centrality of the World Council of Churches as the most effective coordinating base for Protestant efforts in Europe; and 7) the focus of Martin Niemoeller. One notable missing element has to do with Jews as Jews. Jews who had survived the Hitler years did not receive any special treatment but were once again denied an identity, being classified as Displaced Persons (DPs). There was no program for Jews.[1]

The problem of reestablishing contact with the churches and church leadership in Europe must first be seen against the experience at the end of World War I. In his article, "The German Church Since V-E Day" (appearing in *The Living Church*), Henry Smith Leiper describes the Stuttgart Conference of the newly formed *Evangelische Kirche in Deutschland* (EKD).

At the conference, Dutch, British, Norwegian, Swiss, French, Swedish, and American Church leaders sat down with their German brethren. If anyone thinks this is a matter-of-course procedure, let him read the story of 1918-1920 when it took almost two years to restore friendly relations between the German Church leaders and those of the Allied lands.[2]

There seems to have been a special determination by many American Protestant groups that such a mistake would not be made again. As a result, commissions of American Protestant leaders were designated to go to Europe at the earliest possible moment to make contact with their European counterparts and also to assess conditions first hand and report back to the churches and church bodies in America. In addition, European churchmen were brought to the United States in the early spring of 1945 to tell the story of the plight of their churches, before the war in Europe was ended.

The motivation underlying these discussions was expressed quite early in two forms. Samuel McCrea Cavert, in an article "Hunger of Body and Soul: Christians of America Must Demonstrate Their Christianity In Healing Fellowship With Christians of Europe," said,

> No more strategic question faces American Christians today than what they are to do to help the Christians of the Continent of Europe the moment hostilities are over. It is not a problem that can be referred to a political organization like the UNRRA...; but there will be a more distinctive service, of a more personal character, to be rendered by the Christian agencies. For they can also minister to the equally insistent needs of the spirit.[3]

The Second National Study Conference of the Commission on a Just and Durable Peace of the Federal Council of Churches of Christ in America met in Cleveland, Ohio, on January 16-19, 1945. Some 450 representatives heard the report of the Commission under the Chairmanship of John Foster Dulles. The lengthy report of the Conference was distributed to the churches for their consideration. It emphasized the "Church of Christ as a world fellowship," then called for "...reconstruction of devastated lands, the rebirth of hope and determination for a world of justice...." Sections of the report referred to the Dunbarton Oaks Proposal in relation to the Thirteen Guiding Principles and the Six Pillars of Peace adopted at earlier meetings of the commission of Just and Durable Peace. A special section of the report was devoted to Germany; another to Japan.

In section III, Recommendations for Action, item 5, the report stated, (in part):

> War-ravaged peoples in many lands will require help in their struggle to reestablish civic order. Basic welfare relief will need to be supplemented by assistance to the churches to reconstitute their services within their local communities in order to become effective centers of vital life and hope. The churches of America are urged to support to the fullest their agencies of relief and reconstruction already in operation in order to assist the churches of other lands in this period of reconstruction.[4]

The churches of America acted. Much evidence can be shown to support this statement. An example follows. As the extent of the need became more clear at the end of the war in Europe, an estimate of the extent of the war damage to Europe's churches was set at $1,700,000,000, in addition to the need for food, clothing, restored theological education, lay workers and leadership throughout Europe.[5] By August, 1945, the commitment of major Protestant denominations was clear: $112,000,000 was pledged for relief purposes: Methodists, $26,000,000; Presbyterians, $27,000,000; Northern Baptists, $14,000,000; Southern Baptists, $10,000,000; Lutherans, $15,000,000; and Congregationalists, $4,500,000. Additionally, non-member churches committed denominational counterparts in Europe. Several U. S. denominations voted in their 1945 annual meetings to make the relief and rehabilitation needs of Europe the first item of business, with priority over denominational need at home.[6]

This commitment is also reflected in what I have listed as point 4 of the major themes noted above. The churches and agencies of the Church in America made their outstanding churchmen available to assist in this effort. The Lutherans sent P. O. Bersell, Ralph H. Long and Lawrence B. Meyer to Europe in March-April, 1945, for on-site visits. Meyer represented the Missouri Synod. Samuel McCrea Cavert, General Secretary of the Federal Council of Churches, was released to serve with the World Council of Churches in the relief and rehabilitation effort. Stewart W. Herman, the last pastor of the American Church in Berlin, was recalled to Europe to be the WCC representative in the field, visiting all parts of Germany and other parts of occupied Europe as soon as they had been secured. Sylvester C. Michelfelder was sent to Geneva to represent all Lutherans assigned to World Council of Churches. G. Bromley Oxnam and Bishop Henry Knox Sherrill made two trips to Europe, the first before the end of the war, the second in November, 1945 with Franklin Clark Fry, of the United Lutheran Church.

Reciprocally, in the Spring of 1945, Marc Boegner, President of the French Protestant Church Federation, Bishop George K. A. Bell of

England and W. A. Visser't Hooft of the World Council of Churches came to the United States in a historic visit. They were joined by American churchmen making presentations in New York City at the Cathedral of St. John the Divine on May 17, 1945. The three men, singly and together also travelled to other parts of the country between May 7 and May 19.

Churchmen on both sides of the Atlantic threw themselves into the task. The names found most frequently constitute the leadership need met in all calls for assistance: from America, A. L. Warnhuis, Henry Smith Leiper, Carl Herman Voss, Robert A. Root, Hugh Thompson Kerr, Ewart E. Turner, Conrad Hoffman, James M. Bader, L. W. Goebel, J. W. Behnken, J. A. Aasgard and a host of American churchmen serving in the Chaplain's Corps stationed in Europe-Stainbrook, Ostergren, Wood, Bailey, et al. In Europe: Bishop Eivind Berggrav and Ole Hallesby of Norway, Alphonse Koechlin of Switzerland, Henrik Kraemer of Holland, Pierre Mavry of France, Karl Barth, J. H. Oldham of London, John Baillie of Scotland and from the World Council of Churches, J. Hutchinson Cockburn, Benjamin J. Bush, Adolf Keller (sent to the U. S.), and Hans Schoenfeld. In Germany the emerging leadership centered in the newly formed Evangelische Kirche in Deutschland (EKD), including Theophilus Wurm, Hans Asmussen, Eugen Geerstenmaier, Hans Meisser, Hans Lilje, Otto Dibelius, Helmuth Thielicke, Heinrich Gruber, Friedrich von Bodelschwingh, Metzenbaum, Menn, Fricke, Mass, and Martin Niemoeller.

Martin Niemoeller emerged from eight years as "Hitlers' prisoner" to find himself an international hero and an unwilling participant in controversy. The religious press published a series of interviews by Oxnam, Dorothy Thompson, and a number of chaplains and other visitors from the U. S. Additionally, the attack on Niemoeller by Rex Stout and the Writers War Board facilitated by Frank Kingdon and Eleanor Roosevelt and supported by elements of the press, was widely reported.[7] Niemoeller's return to active participation in Germany's church life was chronicled, as were his changing views of the needs of German Christians and war-ravaged Germany. His participation in the conferences at Frankfurt, Treysa and Stuttgart, his sermons at Stuttgart and his return to his former church at Dahlem, as well as his role as vice-chairman of the Provisional Council of the newly formed EKD were also reported.[8] The proposal that Niemoeller be invited to visit and speak in the United States received the predictable mixed reaction.

But as visitors arrived from Europe, and as American churchmen visited Europe in official commissions sent by their respective denominations, what did they find, and what did they report? As the fall of 1945, and the winter of 1945-1946 approached, these leaders spoke more and more bluntly of the devastation, the extent of the damages, the homeless, the needs of Europe's children, the lack of food, clothing, medical supplies and services and the sad spector of starvation on a unprecedented scale.   Bersell and Meyer for the Lutherans, Leiper, Cavert, Sherrill, Oxnam, Warnhuis, Stewart Herman, the Mennonites, the Friends, the reports coming from the World Council of Churches all were united in calling for immediate massive assistance, to meet the needs among Europe's refugees (estimated at up to 12,000,000), the needy in the cities, and always the children, especially the new-born.   Estimates were that hardly any child born in late 1945 or early 1946, in some parts of Europe, would live.

Most children born in Germany during the last two years are expected to die, it was reported in Geneva by Dr. Hans Schoenfeld, staff member of the World Council of Churches.   In one town..., 99 of 108 children born have already died. He quoted Bishop Otto Dibelius of Berlin as saying that all babies born during the last 12 months in some parishes he had visited have died.[9]

Schoenfeld then called for food, medicine and, especially, insulin.

This report represents the role and work of the World Council of Churches and its agencies and committees. In a report to American churches, Stewart Herman, after describing his 3,000 mile trip through Germany, and the work of both Protestant and Roman Catholic Churches in assuming welfare and relief work there, then mentioned the increasing recognition of the World Council as the "principal agency" for coordinating visits to Germany, and facilitating relief efforts.[10]

The response of the American churches was massive. Centers for collecting food, clothing and supplies were established. Agencies already in place, Protestant, Roman Catholic and Jewish, announced programs and procedures, including careful instructions as to how to prepare and pack provisions to meet requirements established by the occupying Allied forces. The regulations were often seen as hindering relief efforts because of non-fraternizing restrictions in occupied zones.   Also, distribution in Europe was difficult because no agencies were in place. Gradually, the churches and inter-church agencies in Europe were organized as distribution centers to process the food, clothing and supplies being received. One is left with the feeling of disarray and confusion in making the distribution system work, largely because of the general confusion of the immediate post-war period.

Little is included here about the remaining Concentration Camps and evidence of the massive slave labor system.   This response is chronicled in *So It Was True*, as is the reaction to the dropping of the Atomic Bomb in Japan.[11] Nothing needs to be added to this point save to note the horror and outrage before the evidence about the camps, and the moral outrage and concern over the use of the Bomb.[12]

Finally, what about the Jews? Reports of increasing antisemitism in many parts of Europe — and especially in Poland — were noted, but very few Protestant periodicals even mentioned this. Those periodicals most concerned about Jews, such as the *Hebrew Christian Alliance Quarterly*, reported the most information. An article, "Resurgence of Anti-Semitism in Liberated Europe" reports the killing of Jews in Poland, anti-Jewish demonstrations in France with anti-Jewish slogans and signs of antisemitism evident in other parts of Europe.[13] But, to reiterate, there was no program for Jews as Jews; they lost their identity within the designation Displaced Persons or refugees and, in spite of the now well-known Harrison report to President Truman, widely publicized and clearly stating that what had happened to Jews under the Nazis required special consideration, little or nothing specifically for Jews was reported in 1945 in the Protestant press.[14] The title of Professor David Wyman's book, *The Abandonment of the Jews* might well serve as the final word for 1945, forty years after.

Chapter IX Endnotes

1. See: Robert W. Ross, "DP's, Refugees, The Allies and the Jews, 1945-1950" (unpublished mss), and Leonard Dinnerstein, *America and the Survivors of the Holocaust* (New York): Columbia University Press, 1982.

2. Henry Smith Leiper, "The German Church Since V-E Day," *The Living Church* (November 11, 1945): 12.

3. Samuel McCrea Cavert, "Hunger of Body and Soul: Christians of America Must Demonstrate Their Christianity in Healing Fellowship With Christians of Europe," *The Messenger* (March 6, 1945): 11-14.

4. "The Churches and the World Order," *The Christian Century* (February 7, 1945): 174-177, 191.

5. "Plan Needed for Church Reconstruction," *The Christian Century* (May 30, 1945): 645.

6. "Protestants Set Goals for Postwar Relief," *The Christian Century* (August 15, 1945): 940; "Presbyterians Vote to Aid Others First," *The Christian Century* (September 26, 1945): 1084.

7. "Why Attack Niemoeller?" *The Christian Century* (September 12, 1945): 1031-1033, an editorial explaining in detail the reasons for the attack, and essentially refuting them as unfounded. There were others, but many letters to the Editor in the *Century* and in other religious periodicals continued to be skeptical of Niemoeller.

8. "German Prostestantism to Stress Social Action," *The Lutheran Standard* (October 13, 1945): 15; this same report, prepared by the *Religious News Service*, appeared in a number of religious periodicals in the Fall of 1945.

9. "World Council Hears Report on German Mortality Rate," *The Messenger* (October 16, 1945): 23.

10. "Clergyman Reports on Activity of German Church," *Loc. Cit.*

11. Benjamin B. Ferencz, *Less Than Slaves* (Harvard University Press, 1979): p. 187, cites a Federal Republic of Germany report for 1977, identifying 1,634 subcamps, which does not include the main Concentration Camps that were administrative centers for the Forced Labor system.

12. See, Robert W. Ross, *So It was True: The American Protestant Press and the Nazi Persecution of the Jews* Minneapolis, MN (University of Minnesota Press, 1980): pp. 203-257.

13. "Resurgence of Anti-Semitism of Liberated Europe"; "More Jews Have Survived in Europe Than Was Thought Possible": "15,000 Jewish Orphans Biggest Problem for French Jews": *The Hebrew Christian Alliance Quarterly* (Summer, 1945): 24-26.

14. "Jews Are Saddest People Among Displaced Persons; They Have No Place to Go," *Loc. Cit.*

Chapter X

SURVEYING HOLOCAUST ATTITUDES: FORTY YEARS AFTER

Jutta Bendremer

Revisionist literature is being pandered about with gusto by such antisemitic publishers as The Noontide Press in Torrance, California and The Institute of Historical Review located in the same city. The Institute publishes quarterly its *Journal of Historical Review*, a pseudo-scholarly offering which features such titles as "The Mechanics of Gassing," "The International 'Holocaust' Controversy" and "The Fake Photograph Problem." The Noontide Press book list cites the following among its offerings: *Did Six Million Really Die?*, *The Hoax of the 20th Century* and *Debunking the Genocide Myth*.

I felt, for a number of reasons, that a survey of knowledge about, and attitudes towards, the Holocaust to be a worthwhile undertaking.

Vituperative literature is readily available to the American public; the world press informs us with great regularity of the bombing of a synagogue or a march by neo-Nazis; magazine-format TV exposes millions of viewers to intimate scenes of brown-shirted neo-Nazi groups busily (and happily) engaged in feasting, drilling and peddling copies of *Mein Kampf*, surrounded by all the paraphernalia of the Hitler decade; antisemitism, an ever present menace, seems to be more visible again. At the same time, Holocaust studies are accelerating on campuses throughout the United States at an unprecedented pace. At present over 200 colleges and universities are offering courses which deal with the Holocaust. Books, plays, articles and conferences are proliferating. The Holocaust, some educators feel, has become a fad; others maintain that funds for Holocaust memorials could be used to greater advantage to underwrite studies in Judaica. Some Jewish theologians contend that there is too much talk about the Holocaust; others say there is too little, and what is being said and taught is incorrect. This survey was devised to measure, in a random sampling of some 200 people in a large midwestern city of 500,000, just how much each respondent knew about the Holocaust, how he/she had obtained that information and how such information should be used today. There were fourteen questions on the survey. Some required multiple-choice answers; some requested a write-in answer. Almost all respondents chose to submit some personal data on age, occupation, education, sex and ethnic background. In developing the questionnaire, I tried to work from Michael Berenbaum's philosophic approach, summed up in these words:

> ...[We] should aim for a living memorial, not just a physical memorial — a legacy of teaching, learning and scholarship, a memorial that responds to the needs of the living, that takes the memory of those who died and uses it to inform our lives.

A summary of the major findings of this investigation is briefly presented below.

Question 1: Briefly define Holocaust.

Answer D: Holocaust refers to the systematic extermination of Jews by Nazis.

In analyzing the raw data from the survey I found, quite predictably, that 88% of all the respondents felt that answer D in question 1 defined the Holocaust most succinctly. Females tended to select answer D slightly more frequently than did males (91% females — 87.3% males). When I viewed this response from the perspective of the ethnic background of the sample, I found that 66.7% of people of "other" backgrounds also chose answer D to define the Holocaust. (In the text, "other" backgrounds refers to those not included in Anglo-Saxon, German, Italian, East European, Hispanic, Black, American, "Heinz 57" or no response.) Understandably 100% of the subjects of German origin chose answer D, while only 50% of Hispanics chose that answer. When this response was measured in terms of the religious background of the subjects, I found that Catholics, Jews and atheists were more likely to agree with answer D. It was interesting to note that only 50% of the Protestant sample chose answer D while the other 50% chose answer C (Holocaust refers to the invasion of Poland).

Questions 2-6 dealt mainly with knowledge about the Holocaust and how such information had been obtained, but no significant data emerged to indicate strong trends. Results were scattered over the spectrum of possible responses. This may be attributed to the lack of public or parochial education dealing with the events of the Holocaust. However, it was noted in questions 2 and 8 that the majority of respondents "agreed" or "strongly agreed" that the Nazis directed their hatred not only towards

Jews, but also towards Gypsies, Communists, Socialists, the feeble-minded and the criminally insane.

Question 7: There is a dangerously large number of people in America today who are Nazis or who are philosophically in agreement with Nazi doctrine.

Answer: Continuum — A Strongly agree — F Strongly disagree

Some interesting results were obtained in analyzing the responses to this question. Over 65% of the respondents felt that neo-Nazism is ubiquitous and extremely threatening to our society. Although there seemed to be majority consensus that neo-Fascist activity exists, well-educated professionals viewed this as less dangerous than did poor and black people.

Just as there has been a reemergence of neo-Nazi activity in this and many other countries, so has there been an unprecedented flow of Holocaust information through the media.   The TV mini-series *The Holocaust* drew millions of viewers, including 68% of the respondents (Question 9), who watched either part or all of it. There was little differentiation between the sexes in viewing part of the TV show; however, females tended, in greater numbers, to watch the show in its entirety.

Question 10:   Whom should the world hold responsible for the Holocaust? You may circle more than one.

In answering Question 10 the majority felt Germany alone or Europe was responsible for the Holocaust.   When dividing the respondents into ethnic and religious affiliations, I found that Germans and Italians felt that Germany and Europe shared equal responsibility, while Eastern Europeans, Hispanics, Anglo-Saxons and Americans felt Germany alone was responsible for the Holocaust. Catholics and Jews seemed to be evenly split in assigning responsibility for the Holocaust to "Germany and other countries," while Protestants felt "other" nations were more responsible.

Question 11: What factors were responsible for the Holocaust? Circle the three most important

Answer: B. lack of Jewish resistance to the gradual elimination of their rights.

E. unwillingness on the part of the entire world to believe the Nazi Masterplan and its methods of implementation.

F. government promoted policy of rampant anti-Semitism in Germany.

Respondents were asked to identify the three factors they felt were more responsible for the Holocaust. More than 50% felt that answer E —

the world's unwillingness to believe the Nazi Masterplan—was the overriding reason for the Holocaust. Over 33% were college-educated respondents. The second most popular choice was answer B. A total of 44%, including technical, trade and high school educated survey participants, felt that one of the primary causes for the Holocaust was the lack of Jewish resistance to the gradual elimination of their rights. The third answer chosen most frequently was F. It was interesting to note that religious differences seemed related to the wide divergence of answers.

Question 12: Do you feel that the study of the Holocaust should be included in American public education? Yes   No

If yes, circle the three most important reasons.

Answer:

A. to prevent a potential future Holocaust.

B. to increase the awareness of the effects of propaganda.

D. to become aware of the magnitude of the effect unleashed and unbridled government supported prejudice would have on other groups and societies.

For Question 12, an overwhelming 91% of survey participants answered that the study of the Holocaust should be included in American public education.   Respondents' answers suggested that widespread Holocaust education should exist not only to learn what happened to six million Jews between 1933 and 1945, but also to protect themselves and society from unbridled, excessive governmental control and prejudice. Moreover, it may well be that Holocaust courses are being taught in the parochial or public school sector which may not be disseminating the information that this survey indicated most people want from such a study. It is possible that by overemphasizing only what happened to the Jews (physical and mental atrocities) one may be missing the opportunity to give the individual who takes such a course the understanding and awareness of how government-instigated propaganda techniques and societal prejudices are manipulated to enslave or annihilate the unwary.   Most respondents agreed that there is a glaring need to identify potential threats to personal and collective freedoms and to guard against such threats in the future.

Perhaps the most unsettling result of this survey is the apparent inability of the better-educated respondent to exhibit sensitivity to the potential danger of totalitarian propaganda.   Our system of education needs to explore the reasons why this situation, as indicated by the survey, exists.

Although the uniqueness of this watershed event cannot be sufficiently stressed, my research suggests that to teach the Holocaust effectively, it is important to integrate its historical origins with present-day political events and trends. Isolating and identifying the life-threatening dangers of political manipulation in the hands of skillful despots may serve as one of the bases for class discussion and should provide commonalities for all ethnic groups. I believe that such an approach would help to sensitize students to the danger of the kinds of political rhetoric used throughout the world today which, left unchecked, might have results which closely parallel or even exceed those in Germany during the Holocaust years.

Another area of study closely allied to the preceding is that which deals with propaganda techniques. Most Holocaust courses scrutinize the virulent propaganda campaigns used so successfully by Germany specifically against the Jews, quite unaware that similar tactics are employed by our own multi-faceted media. Successful advertising is a form of propaganda, not necessarily political, but manipulative, seductive and vastly appealing to all segments of society. Making students aware of the inherent dangers in advertising propaganda, helping them to recognize other sources of propaganda—for example appeals by special interest groups or the removal of books considered immoral (Huxley's *Brave New World*, Malamud's *The Fixer*) from the shelves of public school libraries—would also aid them to become more critical, more independent thinkers. It is necessary to impress on students that Germans from all walks of life, from menial laborers to philosophers, succumbed almost en masse to "right thinking" propaganda.

Another topic for exploration in any Holocaust course is the one which deals with concentration camp mentality. The philosophy that urges society to put people away for their own good or for the good of society is similar to that used by the Nazis: first to isolate, then exterminate mental defectives, physically handicapped, minority groups, political dissidents and, of course, six million Jews. Brainwashing people into believing that certain individuals or groups threaten them or society and therefore must be incarcerated or eliminated is a tactic still widely used today. The story of Jacob Timmerman, the Argentinian editor-in-chief of the liberal newspaper *La Opinion*, provides an excellent case in point. Timmerman was incarcerated and cruelly tortured—as were other "political enemies"—for thirty months. He survived, sought asylum in Israel for a while, and has recently resumed his career as a crusading journalist. Others were not as fortunate.

The Holocaust is not a dead issue. It is a viable area of study which has many implications for the world today. It provides society with a living memorial of man's potential for destruction, the ease with which such destruction can be accomplished and the need to sensitize humankind to the signals that produce danger. Dedicated, well-trained teachers share in the responsibility to educate an often uninformed, apathetic public. Only then can we hope to challenge society into an awareness of its own motives, into thinking and rethinking issues which affect its ability to survive with the basic rights and freedoms for all its citizens intact. The Holocaust remains a living reminder to all people:

those who refuse to abandon their liberties at any price as well as to those who willingly relinquish such freedoms for the sake of misplaced loyalties, excessive hedonism or the clarion call of false messiahs.

Chapter XI

DIETRICH BONHOEFFER AND THE JEWS: AN AGENDA FOR EXPLORATION AND CONTEMPORARY DIALOGUE

F. Burton Nelson

The theme of "Dietrich Bonhoeffer and the Jews" continues to be important for research, dialogue and reflection among Jews and Christians. Bonhoeffer's own writings, the oral histories of those who knew him in the flesh, documentation newly brought to light, correspondence during the time of the Church Struggle — all of these can assist in casting light on the role that he played, and continues to play, in the ongoing story of Jewish-Christian relationships.

In this paper I consider three sections: the literature thus far; the precise Holocaust context in which Bonhoeffer lived, thought, and wrote; and a suggested agenda for further exploration and scholarship.

I. *The Literature Thus Far*

A growing body of literature is taking shape that provides a focus on Dietrich Bonhoeffer and the Jewish People. Several of these are cited here.

1. One of the truly significant and substantial essays is Eberhard Bethge's "Dietrich Bonhoeffer and the Jews," a detailed and insightful paper which was initially presented at an International Bonhoeffer Symposium at Oxford University in 1980.[1] Bethge's biography is, and will continue to be, the definitive account of the life and legacy of Bonhoeffer, but this essay moves us substantially beyond the biography in the subject area under consideration. He makes the point that prior to the essay there had been no thoroughgoing study of the history of the relationship between Bonhoeffer and the Jews. He does cite the studies of Armin Boyens and Wolfgang Gerlach who have examined the relationship of the Confessing Church and the ecumenical movement to the Jewish people; the picture is given in these studies of Bonhoeffer as an active representative from Christian perspectives.

Bethge also refers to the work of Richard Guthridge, a British scholar who wrote *The German Evangelical Church and the Jews*, which has sections on the role of Bonhoeffer. He further refers to the study of Eva Fleischner, *Judaism in German Christian Theology Since 1945*. Others noted are William Peck, Ruth Zerner, Pinchas Lapide, and Franklin H. Littell.

Bethge is very helpful in contributing a point-by-point account of Bonhoeffer's relationship to Jews: the family friendships, Dietrich's own close Jewish friends, and the family's firm rejection of racist ideology in 1933. A quotation from an unpublished manuscript by Heinz Eduard Todt states Bonhoeffer's views succinctly:

> In 1933 Bonhoeffer was almost alone in his opinions; he was the only one who considered solidarity with the Jews, especially with non-Christian Jews, to be a matter of such importance as to obligate the Christian Churches to risk a massive conflict with the state — a risk which could threaten their very existence.

In 1935, after the passage of the infamous Nuremberg laws, Bonhoeffer's unequivocal position became: "Only he who cries out for the Jews may sing Gregorian chant!" Bethge entertains no doubt that Bonhoeffer's primary motivation for entering the active political conspiracy was the treatment of Jews at the hand of the Nazis.

2. Ruth Zerner, "Dietrich Bonhoeffer and the Jews: Thoughts and Actions, 1933-45."[2]

Professor Zerner frankly admits that there are observations in Bonhoeffer's writings related to Jews and Jewish experiences that contain problematic passages, ambiguities, and even contradictions. Her suggestion is that he was, to a certain extent, a victim of his background and culture; consequently we must take as our primary focus Bonhoeffer's actions rather than his theology in the early years of the Nazi era.

Attention is called to Bonhoeffer's ecumenical initiatives on behalf of the Jews and also his identification with the sufferings of all Jews.

3. Guy C. Carter, "Confession from Bethel, August, 1933: Provisional Draft or Definitive Witness?"[3]

This document, the Bethel Confession, which was produced in the early period of Hitler's era, was quite disappointing in its final form. In the process of discussion and reformulation, it lost its prophetic and provocative edge. The role of Dietrich Bonhoeffer is given in some detail, describing his vision for a new beginning in the Christian Church's attitude toward Jews. He collaborated with Wilhelm Vischer on the chapter, "The Church and the Jews." Because the statement was diluted and modified, however, he ultimately refrained from signing the document.

4. Geffrey Kelly, "Dietrich Bonhoeffer and the Jews: The Possibility of Jewish-Christian Reconciliation."[4]

In this perceptive and penetrating essay, Professor Kelly traces the chronicle of Bonhoeffer's monitoring of the Church's policies and performance, underscoring his own distress and disappointment with the "weak, playing-it-safe" tactics of the Confessing Church. Kelly insists that more than any other spokesperson, Bonhoeffer pointed out that not only must Christians defend Jews, but that the fate of Christianity is linked to the fate of Judaism. In short, to reject Judaism and Christianity's Jewish roots is to reject Christ himself.

These four recent studies do not comprise all the literature which focuses on the theme of Bonhoeffer and the Jews, but they do represent component parts of a growing body of writing.

II. *The Precise Holocaust Context*

It is a fact that almost everything that Dietrich Bonhoeffer wrote is set against the backdrop of the relentless, brutal, barbaric evolution of the Holocaust. If this fact is to be taken seriously, it means that we who are studying, researching and writing about Bonhoeffer must seek to bring together with *much* more precision, *much* more insight, and *much* more accuracy, the connecting links between his theology and the historic chronicle of shame that marked the Holocaust years.

It is regrettable that many of us who study Bonhoeffer seem to be too lax, too uniformed and far too imprecise on the Holocaust context. To keep up with the steady stream of literature and the increasing number of detailed accounts offered by survivors demands sentinel attention. Thus the precise contextual setting of the Bonhoeffer writings — whether essays, books, correspondence, sermons, notes, poems, novels — can frequently offer windows into his thought world, as well as into his meanings.

The point of this contextual approach took on specific significance to me as I became aware of documents among the captured war records from Nazi Germany, the Guertner Diaries. Entered as evidence in the Nuremberg War Crimes Trials, these diary entries were kept during the period that Franz Guertner was the German minister of justice. A summary of the contents follows this description.

The diary entries are summaries of incoming correspondence and reports. They deal with a variety of topics, particularly the involvement of Nazi Party members in criminal activities, and represent a running commentary on injustice and persecution committed by the Nazi regime. Frequent entries include such subjects as the persecution of churches by members of the SA and Hitler Youth, particularly the Confessing Church (*Bekennende Kirche*) and the trial of Pastor Martin Niemoller, restrictions imposed on the Catholic Church, and persecutions of many individual priests and Jehovah's Witnesses. Other items pertain to tortures and mistreatment of individuals in concentration camps and the bypassing of the judicial process by the Gestapo in cases of protective custody. There are entries on sterilization, the eliminating of Jews and political adversaries of the Nazis, and amnesties or quashings of criminal proceedings against party and SA members. Several items are concerned with Julius Streicher and his attacks on individuals. There are many other topics.[5]

The heart of the matter is that this precise, day-by-day chronicle was kept by Hans von Dohnanyi, the brother-in-law of Dietrich Bonhoeffer, and subsequent partner in the underground resistance movement. Von Dohnanyi was a staff member in the Ministry of Justice and had access to the flood of reports which were received almost daily. After his diligent secret recording of these reports, the extent of the documentation was staggering—2,200 pages of single-spaced, typed material! During the mid-thirties Bonhoeffer was privy to the inside story of Nazi barbarism and brutality. He and his brother-in-law were extremely close to each other during those years and knew far more than the average citizen of the Third Reich what was happening.

It is precisely during these years, when behind-the-scenes scraps of information about the persecution and brutal treatment of the Jews, and others, were flowing into the Ministry of Justice, that Dietrich Bonhoeffer was writing the two books that have become, and will continue to be, classics of religious devotion and profound spirituality. *The Cost of Discipleship* (published in 1937) was a product of these years, much of the material given in lectures to the students of the Finkenwalde Seminary, 1935-37. *Life Together*, though written later (published in 1939), reflected the corporate experience of the small Finkenwalde Seminary community in the context of the unfolding Nazi madness.

Clifford Green is surely right when he designates *The Cost of Discipleship* as unmistakably and undoubtedly an autobiographical document from Bonhoeffer's hand.[6]

The precise Holocaust context for all of Bonhoeffer's writings after his two dissertations should shed light on the evolution of his thoughts and perspectives, including his relationship to the Jews and the reference in his books and essays to the Jews. An illustration of this is the well-known dictum of Bonhoeffer's, "Only he who cries out for the Jews may sing Gregorian chants." As previously stated, Eberhard Bethge now dates this statement at the end of 1935, the precise time of the infamous Nuremberg laws. The precise Holocaust context of the shout deepens the importance and the profundity of its message.

III. *An Agenda for Further Exploration and Scholarship*

The quest for further understanding of "Dietrich Bonhoeffer and the Jews" is underway, but much remains to be done.[7] At least seven areas can be identified for further exploration, research, and involvement.

1. Members of "the Bonhoeffer Guild," those who pursue the study of Bonhoeffer's life and work in scholarly endeavor, will be benefited by a growing and increasing participation in Holocaust research, and inter-disciplinary approaches. There is a foundational need to become much more

precise in the Holocaust context as it shaped the responses Bonhoeffer made in life and word on behalf of the Church Struggle, as well as his own grappling with the demands of Christian discipleship.[8]

2.   A plausible way to develop this heightened precision about the Holocaust is to become more directly and substantially involved in the contemporary Jewish-Christian dialogue, including colloquia with both Jewish and Christian scholars and leaders.[9]

3.   Doctoral dissertations offer superb opportunities for researching a well-defined subject area, especially related to Bonhoeffer and the Holocaust or to Jewish-related themes.

4.   All the articles and essays, as well as scattered passages throughout the corpus of his writings, that Bonhoeffer wrote relating to the Jews should be brought together within one volume. An introduction, accompanied by brief commentary, for each entry would be immensely useful and provocative.

5.   Surely one of the key figures in the Bonhoeffer saga was his brother-in-law, Hans von Dohnanyi. A full-length biography, together with resource documentation, is awaited. A member of Franz Guertner's Department of Justice staff in the 1930s and a staff member of the Ah-mehr later, von Dohnanyi served as a perennial conduit for Bonhoeffer's detailed grasp of Holocaust events. Bonhoeffer and he were extremely close. The personal journal that von Dohnanyi kept while he was a prisoner of the Nazis should eventually be published.

6.   The Guertner Diaries of 1934-38 (or selections from them), "The Chronicle of Shame," should be translated and published. Bonhoeffer had access to the massive details of the Nazi treatment of the Jews and other victims through his brother-in-law, Hans von Dohnanyi.

7.   One by one the eyewitnesses to Bonhoeffer, to his family, to the underground resistance, and to the Holocaust at large are passing from the scene. Oral histories are imperative for extending the "Bonhoeffer and the Jews" theme, as well as innumerable other aspects of his life and times.[10]

This suggested agenda for exploring further the "Dietrich Bonhoeffer and the Jews" motif is both specific and achievable. I am hopeful that in the next five year period most of the goals will have been reached.

Chapter XI Endnotes

[1.] Eberhard Bethge, "Dietrich Bonhoeffer and the Jews," in John D. Godsey and Geffrey B. Kelly, editors, *Ethical Responsibility: Bonhoeffer's Legacy to the Churches* (Toronto Studies in Theology, Vol. 6) (Lewiston: The Edwin Mellen Press, 1981), pp. 43-96.

[2.] *Jewish Social Studies*, Summer/Fall, 1975, Vol. XXXVII, Nos. 3-4, pp. 235-250.

[3.] A paper presented at the Fourth International Bonhoeffer Symposium at Hirschluch bei Storkow in East Germany in June, 1984. Dr. Carter's dissertation at Marquette University gave particular focus to the background and development of the Bethel Confession. The material will be published.

[4.] A paper presented at the Scholars' Conference on the Church Struggle and the Holocaust in New York, March, 1983. The material will become available shortly in a collection of papers given at the Scholars' Conferences, published by the Edwin Mellen Press.

[5.] National Archives Microfilm Publications: Records of the United States Nuremberg War Crimes Trials, Guertner Diaries (October 5, 1934- December 24, 1938), p. 3. The United States National Archives is a repository of over ten million captured war documents. The original Guertner Diaries are kept in the Archives, as are all documents used in the Nuremberg Trials as evidence.

[6.] See the insightful volume by Clifford J. Green, *Bonhoeffer: The Sociality of Christ and Humanity* (Missoula, Montana: Scholars Press, 1972), especially pp. 177-200, "*Nachfolge* and the Autobiography of its Theology."

[7.] Eberhard Bethge has called attention to the fact that "on the German side there is as yet no thoroughgoing study of the history of the relationship between 'Bonhoeffer and the Jews.'" (See page 46 of the essay cited in Note #1.) His essay is a monumental contribution to the larger project.

[8.] A new "Bonhoeffer Reader" is in process, edited by Professor Geffrey Kelly and F. Burton Nelson. It is anticipated that all the selections will be set in the context of time and place, and that a detailed chronological calendar will show the connections between Bonhoeffer's writings and the evolving events of the Church Struggle and the Holocaust.

9. A prime example of this involvement is Eberhard Bethge in West Germany. He has been a leader in the Jewish-Christian dialogue, including steps taken by the Protestant Church to promote study and discussion in the congregation.

10. The current video oral history project of Professor J. P. Kelley of Lynchburg College deserves wholehearted encouragement and support. Others known to have participated in the quest for oral histories include: Professor Michael Ryan of Drew University; Professor Ruth Zerner of Lehman College, City University of New York; Mary Glazener of Central, South Carolina; Bain Boehlke and Gerald Drake of Trinity Films; actor David Soul of Westlake California; and Professor F. Burton Nelson, North Park Theological Seminary, Chicago.

Chapter XII

HAVE GERMAN PROTESTANTS LEARNED THEIR LESSONS FROM HISTORY?

Wolfgang Gerlach

"Forty years after" is a biblical anniversary *sui generis*. The Bible uses the number "forty" to indicate a long difficult path in the life of an individual or a people as a whole. Forty is the symbol for purification and ripening between God's nearness and being God-forsaken. "Forty years after" sounds different in Germany than in America. "Forty years after Auschwitz" implies a question: How ripe have we become, as Germans and as Christians, in Germany? I am a full participant in this forty year evaluation, having been born in 1933, but I am afraid forty years is too short a time for a people to mature. And for what, one could ask, should they ripen?

The following declarations and propositions for theologians, synods, and individual work groups in Protestant Germany will demonstrate what maturation process is continuing. In 1980, the Synod of the Church of the Rhineland formulated a resolution which I believe to be the most significant step taken by a Church in Germany in this century. The essence and intent of that resolution—called "repentance and renewal"—is as follows:

first, the turning away from the doctrine which enabled the Church to disinherit Israel, and a turning toward a common theology of promise and hope;

secondly, the turning away from any Christian triumphalism and a turning toward the revelation that "the Jewish documentation of suffering and the history of the suffering of Jesus Christ are inseparable;"

and thirdly, the turning away from the anti-Jewish interpretation of the New Testament, and a turning toward a
common witnessing of faith by Jews and Christians, with
the aim of accepting common responsibility for the world.

The seven propositions formulated by the Rhineland Synod in 1980
are cast into the form of confessions; i. e., the confession of co-responsibility and guilt for the Holocaust, the confession of the Hebrew Bible as
the basis for faith connecting Jews and Christians, and the confession of
"Jesus Christ, the Jew, who is the Messiah of Israel and thus the saviour of
the world." The term in German language, "Messias Israels," suggests the
term "Messiah *for* Israel." This misunderstanding would evoke a renewed
fear of proselytizing ("Judenmission") among Jews and would give Christians a justification for converting Jews. The formula of compromise — as
I see it — would be to understand "Messias Israels" as "Messiah of Israel,"
in the sense of "out of Israel." This Messiah derives from the root which
supports pagan Christians (see Paul's Epistle to the Romans, c. 11:18,
which is the explicit motto of the confession of the Rhineland Synod).

Several weeks after the resolution of the Rhineland Synod, thirteen
professors from the Theological Seminary in Bonn responded with "Con-
siderations of the Synod Resolution for the Renewal of Relations between
Christians and Jews." Within their statement, they expressed "considerable theological reservations" with regard to a "confusing and indis-
criminate terminology;" condescendingly, they saw their task as one of in-
structing the Christians of the Rhineland Synod.

"The Jew as such has no guarantee of salvation," they wrote. To Gentiles the "salvation of freedom from the Law given in Christ" is granted.
Of the Jews, Paul has testified: "That is true. They were broken off (like
branches of a tree) because of their unbelief, but you stand fast only
through faith" (Romans 11:20). The professors in Bonn saw the situation
according to the classic formula: the Jews have fallen into error and faith-
lessness, and Christians alone are the keepers of the true faith. "Torah-
Judaism and belief in Christ are therefore separate, distinct and irreconcil-
able."

A second spirit inspired the Bonn document. Its authors are led not
only by an attitude of theological hardness of heart, but by a spirit of historical impenitence as well. They refuse, as Christians, to accept — *espres-
sis verbis* — guilt for the crimes of the National Socialists, on the grounds
that, indeed, "the National Socialist ideology was just as clearly
unChristian as it was anti-Christian and anti-Jewish."

Helmut Gollwitzer and Berthold Klappert take issue with the Bonn
theologians, criticizing their absolute refusal to make an historical event —
the Holocaust — an integral factor in their theological thinking. The
Catholic theologian Johann Baptist Metz, of Munster in Westfalia, has ad-

vised his students: Ask yourself if the theology you are getting to know is such that it could actually be the same *before* and *after* Auschwitz. If so, then regardless of whatever name it may be associated with, leave it alone!

For those in Bonn, Christendom is "guiltless" in the Holocaust and therefore rid of any blame. The repression of this Christian complicity and co-responsibility in the Holocaust renders "repentance and renewal" impossible and fixes the famous and horrible image of the blindfolded Synagogue in opposition to the radiant all-seeing Ecclesia in the Strasbourg Cathedral. "Millions of people have died at the hands of this Christian triumphalism, with its pretended right perception of God, the right faith and the new division of humanity into the Chosen and Unchosen" (Gollwitzer and Klappert, ibidem. DS Nr. 37, v. 14.9,1980).

The Bonn theologians profess an historical theology that should, unchanged, remain valid for all time, with all the signs of classic Christian orthodoxy. The Holocaust remains irrelevant in the Bonn theology: etsi Auschwitz non daretur (as if it never happened). Martin Honnecker, one of the thirteen and their ghostwriter, in a polemical response to my article in the *Deutsches Allgemeines Sonntagsblatt* (no. 4, January 25, 1981), declared correctly: "The real question concerns the authority and binding character of the New Testament witness." And thus, the Protestant interpretation of Scripture is called into question. That, however, would be going too far, so he shrugs his shoulders, asking: "What meaning does Auschwitz have for the Christian faith? Was Christian faith substantially changed by Auschwitz? Evil existed before Auschwitz, too."

I think that here—consciously or unconsciously—he has reached a high degree of cynicism. That is to say, in Honnecker's view, Auschwitz *must* not *necessarily* and indeed *should* not have any special weight for theological reflection. Honnecker sees nothing of the orgy of evil that was begun in the name of Christianity and not least of all in the name of the reformer, Martin Luther. Honnecker refuses to accept that what has been, up to now, a *Jewish* question should become a *Christian* question.

At this same time, Franz Hesse, a professor of Old Testament at the University of Münster, published a letter criticizing the Rhineland Synod resolution in which he revived the terms and views of conventional anti-Judaism. He reproached the Synod for having allegedly refuted the New Testament conviction that the Jews "have missed salvation if they do not believe in the crucified and resurrected Christ as their Saviour and Redeemer." Hesse claimed—as has the present German Chancellor—that succeeding generations should be excluded from co-responsibility and liability for the Holocaust. The younger generations should be spared continual confrontation with this guilt. The sins of the fathers should not be visited upon the children to the third and fourth generation. Hesse argued that the God of the Jews, who was constantly changing in relation to His people, no longer can be seen as the God of the Christians. So Hesse drew the appropriate conclusion by asking a question, the answer to which he could by no means accept: "Is it to be understood, therefore, in the logic of the Synod's statement, that Paul was the first link in a disastrous chain that ended with Auschwitz?" According to Franz Hesse, since the Auschwitz crime may in no way be traced back to Paul, and since Paul has been the guarantor for Christian theology since the Reformation epoch, the significance of the Holocaust must be relativized.

Precisely at this point, post-Holocaust Christian theology must make an important decision; if I canonize Paul within his conventional reception, then the Holocaust becomes irrelevant (or may I say "adiaphorous?"). If I take the Holocaust seriously, Paul's pedestal begins to crumble.

Yet another contribution on the topic of the Rhineland Synod Resolution was issued in 1980, this one from members of the Heidelberg Theological Seminary. They greeted warmly the Resolution's opening with a "startled confession of co-responsibility and guilt on the part of German Christendom in the Holocaust." They also affirmed the goal of the Resolution to reestablish "the confession to God as Creator and Saviour by Christians and Jews alike." The validity of the Jews remaining God's Chosen People would annul the concept of Christians proselytizing the Jews.

They continued: "The Christians should make the Jews jealous by their faith in the God of Israel" (quoting Romans 11:11). In the context of a similar statement made at the Baden Synod in 1980, Rabbi Albert Friedlander is said to have responded: "I am always jealous, but at the moment I don't feel it" (cit. by Peter v. d. Osten-Sacken, *Bericht aus den Arbeitsgruppen zum Thema 'Juden und Christen'* vom 18.5, 1984 für die Berlin – Brandenburgische Synod, S. Ms.).

For the renewal of Christian-Jewish relations, according to the Heidelberg theologians, it is necessary that we Christians listen to and tolerate Jewish objections. Even more, it is desirable that the Jewish objections themselves be reformed time and again. Consequently, the conflicts contained in the New Testament may not yet be considered resolved. These scholars see behind Bonn's refusal to recognize a Christian co-responsibility in the Holocaust a regression to a position antedating the era of the Stuttgart Confession of Guilt in 1945. The Heidelberg group shares with the Rhineland Synod Resolution a theological openness that is not interested in slamming dogmatic emergency brakes, but rather seeks to explore and interpret the Scriptures anew with the Jews in the context of a common and sometimes tragic history.

A statement was made by the Church leaders of the United Evangelical Lutheran Church of Germany (VELKD: Vereinigte Ev. Luth/Kirche Deutschlands) on Christian-Jewish relations (dated 3 June 1983, according to the original text; see in VELKD 23/1983, pp. 4-7). This contribution confesses "co-responsibility and guilt" in the Holocaust and regrets the Churches' silence in regard to the persecution of Jews during the National Socialist era. They do not support the rejection theory and see

their brothers and sisters separated in Christ as having a common in-
heritance. Although, on the whole, this paper expresses a spirit of general
humanity, an insight into the necessity of a theological reevaluation is
lacking. They regret antisemitism, speak out against hatred and animosity
toward Jews and propose a theological work to improve the relations between Christians and Jews. However, it all sounds more like a cosmetic
treatment of symptoms than a real cure.

I have referred to another VELKD study, published a few years earlier, "What Everyone Should Know About Judaism." On the one hand, its
general approach is, in itself, a little weak. Instead of saying; search to
see which causes for the Holocaust could be uncovered within Christian
faith itself, I read between the lines more of the following attitude;
broaden your knowledge of Jewish rituals and terms, so you can be nice to
the Jews! That is, as I see it, a clever and skillful strategy for avoiding the
real problem. The study concludes with a humanitarian prayer for good
relations between Israel and her neighbors.

The Regional Synod of the Evangelical Church of Baden (May 1984)
is, in the letter and spirit of their declaration, relatively close to the
Rhineland Resolution. Just as the New Testament neither detracts from
the Old Testament nor annuls it, "Israel's chosenness is not cancelled by
the choice of the Church from among Jews and the Gentiles" (or, "the
Church consisting of Jews and Gentiles"). At this point, the situation of
Jewish Christians is worthily addressed.

The confession of co-responsibility and guilt in the Holocaust on the
part of Christians in Germany is followed by three statements, by way of
conclusion:

> We *confess with the Jews* God as Creator of Heaven and
> Earth.
> *We believe with the Jews* that Justice and Love are God's in-
> structions for our whole lives. [And I add, at this point the
> Christian tradition according to which Love would be sole-
> ly Christian property is rejected!]
> We *hope with the Jews* for a new Heaven and Earth and
> want to work with them, empowered by this hope for Jus-
> tice and Peace in this world.

These sentences draw partially upon the Rhineland's Resolution.

The Baden Synod avoids characterizing Jesus as "the Messiah of Israel." Instead, they note, "with pain and grief" that "to us Christians, the
confession to the Saviour of the world, crucified and resurrected for one
and all, separates us from the faith of the Jewish people." I ask myself; is
this "pain" an accommodating compromise toward those who would still
prefer to make all Jews Christians? Or is a secret compassion concealed
in this "pain" for those who, unfortunately, still have not realized whose

side Truth is on? Does this "pain" not serve as a facade for the old belief that salvation is a distinctly Christian domain? Why otherwise would they feel "pain" at all? The Baden Synod also omits any mention of the State of Israel, unlike the Rhineland Synod, which declared: "The continuing existence of the Jewish people, its return to the land of promise and creation of the State of Israel are signs of God's faithfulness to His people."

Theses on the theme "Us and the Jews-Israel and the Church"

In 1984, the Reformed Alliance (*Der Reformierte Bund*) celebrated its centennial with regard to the 50th anniversary of Barmen. This date unifies the Alliance by means of seven theses, each of which is explained by a Calvinist theologian. One should certainly say that these theses go much further than the Rhineland's Statement. They are substantially more open in their formulation and venture boldly to the roots of Christian faith, led by the spirit of "encounter and reconciliation" and determined not to give ground to Christian theology in areas where it has sinned.

I.   "From Christians there went out into the world of the Gentiles a seed of hatred toward the Jews, which brought about murder and destruction. This tradition did not get rid of its efficiency and remains evident in the Church and theology today."

II. Contrary to the Christian mode of speaking which, at any rate, concedes a little of God's salvation to the Jews, Christians are here portrayed as "human beings from the world of the Gentiles," whose "origins were far from the God of Israel and His people." We are "made worthy and are called to participation in the election and in the community of God's covenant originally promised to Israel." The former terminology of "rejected and disinherited Israel" is superseeded by a common ground and points of contact between the divided peoples.

III. Note is made of the nearness of Christians to the Jews on the basis of the first commandment, and the common monotheistic dimension it affirmed. I wonder whether by citing I Corinthians 8:6 we have dealt fully with the suspicion (expressed by some Jews) that we have foresaken monotheism by virtue of the Trinitarian doctrine:

"Yet for us there is one God, the Father, from whom are all things and for whom we exist, and one Lord, Jesus Christ, through whom all things are, through whom we exist."

(In the commentary, Hans-Joachim Kraus is quoted: "God is the Creator, Christ the Mediator of Creation and Saviour. This is the unmistakable foundation on which the Christian community stands, by virtue of which it serves in this world as witness and messenger of the One God.")

IV.   "Thesis four tries to confess the Messiah, formulated in such a way that our call to the Messianic act is thereby included. This thesis attempts to understand *theologically* the Jewish refusal (saying "No" to or rejection) of Jesus as Messiah." (Herman Keller, "Auf dem Weg — Juden und Christen lernen Gottes qute Weisung," in *Hundert Jahre Reformierter Bund. Beiträge zur geschichte und Gegenwart, Bensheim 1984, p. 150.)

V.   Thesis five praises the significance and riches of the Torah for Christians as well as Jews. Reference is made to Jesus, who clearly and unambiguously proclaimed that he had not come to abolish the Law and the Prophets but to fulfill them (Matthew 5:17, 19). Jesus followed the path of Torah in word and deed, to the end.

VI.   In thesis six, the perception is formulated "that the promise of the land is inseparable from the election." Analogous to the Rhineland Synod, it is particularly emphasized that "the Return of Jews to the Homeland is a confirmation of God's loyalty." With this loyalty of God, Christians can merely express solidarity.

VII.   The seventh thesis recommends that branches of interaction should be allowed to grow from the common roots of faith, since both Christians and Jews are "called to fight together for humanity, justice and peace." Only through our action and prayer together does something of the New Heaven and New Earth promise to light in God's creation.

The path of testimony in the world on the part of Christians and Jews for the sake of their common God could be expressed in this triad, waiting-acting-praying (analogous to the word of Bonhoeffer: the task of the church consists in praying and acting in righteousness). This position might be expressed in the legend of Rabbi Chaim of Volozhyn:

Rabbi Chaim of Volozhyn was so wealthy in his good deeds that it was said of him that upon his death, he would be admitted immediately to the "world to come." But Rabbi Chaim refused to enter until he had been assured that all of his students and teachers from the Yeshiva would be admitted as well. In that way, the Rabbi said, the success of the school would not be due to himself but rather would owe its thanks to them all. When that was granted to him, he requested further that all Jews be similarly admitted since, after all, Jewish fathers carried the responsibility for the Torah. But the Rabbi was not satisfied even when this wish was fulfilled. Finally, he claimed that by virtue of the fact that the Gentiles had received the Jews, they also were participants in the Torah. Simply stated, Rabbi Chaim did not want to enter until he had the assurance that all Humanity would be allowed in. He was then told that, for the time being, it would not be possible, since the arrival of the Messiah had not yet been announced. And so Rabbi Chaim refused to go into the "world to come." He is still standing patiently at the entrance and waits, praying for the final salvation of all Humanity.

CONCLUSION

Among Church leaders and, to a certain extent, in professional circles, consideration is being given—on the path between "repentance and renewal"—to the relations of Christians to the Jewish people, their faith and history. These reflections, however, have not yet reached the grassroots level of congregational life, not even in the case of the Rhineland Synod. The Rhineland Synod Resolution is at best for some people a "thorn in the flesh." The majority prefers to remain uninvolved, whether from fear—as in the case of the pious—or from discomfort with the topic, as is generally true of the Liberals. There may come other resolutions from other synods, but the path to (and it is) new learning could become a century of going through the wilderness and one must expect to encounter the desire on the part of many to return to the old antijudaistic stew to which Paul, John, the Church Fathers and Luther have all contributed ingredients.

Many of the delegations and committees in the Christian-Jewish dialogue are going through a time of weariness and resignation. It is certain that their efforts will not all be greeted with open arms or applause; rather, many church leaders will retain their distance toward Christian-Jewish dialogue, not openly but insidiously. One covers the apparent corpse with a veil of silence. Naturally, it is also a difficult challenge to communicate the new orientations and discoveries in worship, services, Christian education and workshops.

A personal note

My studies are at present on the verge of a new understanding of Pauline theology. I have always had a way of avoiding Paul and, similarly, John. Krister Stendahl's book, *Paul among the Jews and Gentiles*, started me on this theme years ago. There is an article from East Germany by Christoph Hinz, that is new to me, "Discovery of the Jews as Brothers and Witnesses" (*in Zeichen der Zeit*, January 1984). The comprehensive point of reference for Hinz is not the doctrine of justification, but rather "the history and God's path of election, which leads to the Jews and, form there, to the Gentiles" (p. 23).

Peter von der Osten-Sacken thinks and inquires in a similar direction ("Zusammenfassender Bericht am 18.5.1984 aus den Arbeitsgruppen zum Thema "Christen und Juden," Berlin). He underscored Romans 11:25-27:

> Lest you be wise in your conceits, I want you to understand this mystery, brethren: a hardening has come upon part of Israel, until the full number of the Gentiles come in, and so all Israel will be saved; as it is written: 'The Deliverer will come from Zion, he will banish ungodliness from Jacob and thus will be my covenant with them when I take away their sins.'

The election of Israel is God's word and promise for all time. But Christians may know as well, that they, themselves, enter the Kingdom of Heaven. "The most abiding thing, then, which Christians must know from Romans 11 is the abiding election of the people of God since the beginning."

Paul said to the Jews what he said of no other people, that they are chosen and will be saved (p. 9). This word of God must indeed be as reliable as God's word to the Gentiles. If Israel's rejection of the Gospel could have as consequences an expulsion, how often would the church herself have been expelled? In this situation, more than in any other, Israel and the Church find themselves in the same boat. We Christians can only rely upon the loyalty of God to the extent that we confess and testify to this same loyalty extended to Israel (p. 10).

In spite of its insufficiency and fragility, we confess our faith in our Holy Christian Church. Can we not say by the same reason, in spite of the fragmentary nature, we perceive in the people of Israel as well as in all other peoples of the world: "I believe Israel to be the People of God, chosen and destined for salvation"?

I think we are moving to maturity through a painful and sometimes frustrating learning and teaching process, on the path through a new wilderness. Perhaps Philadelphia, with its 15th Conference, is a little oasis from which to draw water of hope for the coming days.

Chapter XIII

WHAT GERMAN CHILDREN LEARN ABOUT THE HOLOCAUST IN GERMAN TEXTBOOKS

Walter Renn

This report on what German young people learn about the Holocaust and its related themes is based on an analysis of some 49 textbooks, workbooks and teacher's guides from history, social studies and political science courses taught in the Federal Republic of Germany. Because most German educators consider textbooks to be one of the most significant educational factors in shaping each generation's understanding of its collective past, a close examination of the textbook treatment of the Holocaust and related subjects should tell us something of the attitudes and perceptions of German educators toward that event and the relationship of the German people to it, of their attempts to teach civic responsibility for opposing government injustice and of their efforts to educate students for democracy. Moreover, the examination of the West German textbooks reveals a good deal about the West German's image of themselves and their society in relation to the Nazi past and the crimes committed by the Nazi government in their name more than 40 years ago.

It is my hope that this critique may contribute to the ongoing debate in Germany to improve future textbook treatment of this sensitive and difficult subject. It is also hoped that it may alert American educators to the weaknesses in U. S. textbooks in dealing with negative and disastrous events, not only treatment of the Holocaust, but also such U. S. history themes as the American Indians, slavery, the incarceration of Japanese-Americans during World War II, Viet Nam and Watergate, to name a few of the traumatic experiences often rendered harmless by U. S. history texts.

All West German textbooks treat at least three broad themes in relation to the Holocaust: 1) the antisemitic roots of Nazism; 2) the Nazi persecution of the Jews during the 1930s; and 3) the events of the Holocaust itself. The texts share a largely common perspective and emphasize many of the same aspects of the Holocaust and related themes, so that it has been possible to draw a composite analysis.

Most texts, having evolved through many editions, do not suffer from factual inaccuracies. However, many texts omit various facts and aspects of this complex subject, and no single text may be said to present a detailed treatment. In quantitative coverage, the German texts compare favorably with other nations' textbook depictions of the subject, though the treatment is often little more than a narrative presentation of the major aspects of the subject and its related events.

There is no doubt that German educators at the government and school level clearly perceive a special obligation to treat the Nazi persecutions and Holocaust in the texts and classroom curricula. They make it clear that the genocide was a unique and unparalleled tragedy for the Jewish people. Although other groups of victims are named, it is pointed out that the Jews were the primary targets of Nazi barbarity, and that they were unique in being singled out for genocide.

There is virtually no trace of antisemitism in the 49 textbooks examined, although there are cases of awkward phrasing, and many cases of texts needlessly presenting vicious antisemitic source materials from Nazi or pre-Nazi racial antisemites to portray Nazi racial ideology, a practice which can only perpetuate negative sterotypes in the minds of students. All texts, however, universally condemn the persecution and murder of the Jews as well as every other aspect of Third Reich theory and practice, a condemnation which has brought about the unintended psychological or sociological explanations to help clarify antisemitism.

But large-scale historical events caused by irrationality and social pathology—for instance, the Crusades, the Black Death, the Inquisition, the seventeenth-century witch trials and burnings, the nineteenth-century Russian pogroms and the twentieth-century Armenian massacres and the Holocaust—require examination and explanation using an interdisciplinary approach, something which German texts scarcely undertake.

While the presentation of religious, economic, racial and political motives for antisemitism is clearly necessary for an historically accurate portrayal, these factors do not in themselves convey the important psychological roots of antisemitism. Prejudices are based on motives of insecurity, guilt, projection, scapegoating, resentments, frustrations, envy and greed, which may result in murderous behavior. Some textbooks show signs of a growing awareness of the progress of psychology and sociology in explaining prejudice, and a few texts, indeed, do present partial functional analyses of antisemitism. None, however, interprets antisemitic prejudice as a mental disorder, as a pathological social aberration. No text provides a coherent explanation of the Holocaust based upon the analysis of antisemitism as a serious mental disorder which reached lethal proportions in the Nazi Era. In short, they still skate the surface of the phenomenon.

All texts offer a factually accurate treatment of the persecution of the Jews during the 1930s and include the major stages of the persecutions from 1933 to 1941. These presentations are largely uniform and appear to follow State guidelines. All such accounts describe the major persecutions correctly, but only a few describe the sufferings of the victims. A few texts, it may be said, focus on Jewish children as an effective means of young reader empathy, but no texts emphasize the deprivations, the disabilities or confiscations suffered by German Jews. Such an approach would make it easier for young people to identify with the victims' plight. In particular, the deprivations and humiliations which made Jewish daily life so cruel should be given greater recognition in the texts. In the same manner, the tragedy of Jewish expulsions from Germany and the looting of Jewish property needs greater attention, and the economic motives for anti-semitism need a more thoroughgoing assessment.

The students learn remarkably little about the Jewish people or their history from the texts. The result is a shadowy depiction of the Jewish victims of the Nazi regime. Despite the sympathy expressed by many textbook authors and despite an emphasis in some texts on the sufferings of Jewish children, the young students learn very little about fellow German Jews who were so badly persecuted in the name of the German people.

This deficiency is due perhaps to postwar German repression of the subject, to the neglect of German scholarship to examine German popular attitudes towards Jews—i.e., German-Jewish social history—during the Third Reich, and to continued postwar antisemitism. The detailed examination of German relations with Jews will have to await further research. The results of this new research will add fresh pain as well as some additional cases of unsung German civic courage. The present depiction of German-Jewish relations during the 1930s minimizes the existence of German antisemitism and over-emphasizes German fear of the Nazi regime and the distorting power of propaganda. In the social history of the period, the Germans are portrayed as passive. The texts make little criticism of the conduct or attitudes of Germans during the Third Reich, and many texts characterize the German people as having been horrified and privately condemnatory of Nazi persecutions.

All textbooks depict the mass murders of the Holocaust, but they are frequently brief about the immediate antecedents to the killings. Only a small minority of texts, for example, raise the issue of the Führer's order or the Wannsee conference for planning the genocide. On the other hand, the texts which do treat these aspects leave no doubt that Hitler gave the order for the Holocaust, and some texts include evidence for Himmler's, Goering's and Goebbel's additional culpability.

The textbooks cannot be said to downplay even the most gruesome aspects of the Holocaust itself, but the under-representation of Jewish survivor accounts gives the depictions an air of detachment, almost of remoteness, and are inadequate in their evocation of the historical magnitude and tragedy of this event. The choice of German instead of Jewish eyewitness documentation for every stage of persecution – from ghettoization, transportation, *SS Einsatzgruppen* massacres, concentration camp life to killing centers – leaves a stronger sense of revulsion than of empathy for the victims slaughtered by the Nazis.

The killing process itself – the gassings and cremations – are not omitted from any text, but the depiction is entirely devoid of comment or evaluation. Many authors close the subject by the use of a quotation from an original document to describe the killing process, then proceed with a shocking abruptness to another subject – usually the German resistance. One may imagine the surprise of the young student who has just read Hoess' or Gerstein's terrifying account of mass gassings and cremation, to find the subject dropped, entirely without comment.

While all texts mention a few of the killing centers by name and describe the gassings and cremation, the murders are portrayed almost as if they took place by an automatic process. The texts barely indicate the identities of the perpetrators. Typically, Hitler, Nazi leaders or the SS are cited as the prime culprits responsible for all horrors. Most texts exhibit scant curiosity about the broader circles of complicity involved in the process of murdering millions of men, women and children. The German people are conspicuously dissociated from mention in connection with any aspect of the execution of the Holocaust. The texts do not examine the personnel requirements for an operation involving the murder of six million people. In the same fashion, the role of businesses, bureaucracy or economic and industrial practice in connection with the killings is not discussed in most texts, and treated only incidentally in the rest. A continuing repression is most evident in this inability to examine the role of Germans in the operation of the killing centers.

The texts also exhibit little agreement on the total number of Jews killed in the Holocaust. The figures range from a minimum of 3.6 million to more than 6 million. Despite the recommendations of specialists that the source of figures be cited, few texts do so and only a small portion of books place the figures in a meaningful perspective or comment on the significance of these figures for Jewish or European history.

Textbook reaction to the tragedy of the killing of the European Jews at the hands of the Germans is expressed mainly in terms of concern for Germany's impaired reputation in the world. Intermediate texts, in particular, emphasize how Hitler dishonored the German people. The German people are not held responsible for either the triumph of National Socialism or for its terrible brutality. There is no discussion of the love, admiration and enthusiasm for Hitler and the Nazi Party or acknowledgment that it was the most popular regime in German national history.

The texts reflect the general German view that the Germans do not share in collective guilt for the persecutions of the Holocaust, but that they do, on the other hand, share in a collective liability for the damage done by the Nazi government and an obligation to compensate, insofar as it is materially possible, for the destruction of the Jewish lives and property during the Nazi years. The view is also expressed that those individual Germans who were involved in the crimes should be brought to justice and punished.

Almost all the texts take the view that the Holocaust was a state secret and that the German people did not learn about it until the end of the war. Some texts also point out that knowledge is a function of interest and concern, and that many Germans may not have known of the killing of the Jews for the simple reason that Germans were indifferent to the fate of Jews. The Jewish people were an alien and expendable group to most Germans, which meant that Jews were scarcely a matter of concern and rarely in their thoughts. Cruel indifference rather than guilty knowledge becomes the accusation against most Germans during the Nazi era. Perhaps this point needs greater emphasis in depictions of the Holocaust, for in the contemporary world we find the same kind of indifference to the fate of faraway people about whom we know nothing.

In depicting German resistance, authors generally are pessimistic about the possibility of effective opposition. They take the attitude that nothing could have been done and that resistance would have been futile. The difficulties of opposition in a totalitarian state and the lack of German resistance have led authors to introduce instances of disapproval — which fell far short of attempting to overthrow the regime — as resistance. Few texts discuss and none emphasize the Western tradition of the right of resistance to tyranny and criminal regimes.

The record of resistance to the Nazi regime by other national groups and by Jews is at best sketchy and represented in only a few texts. On the other hand, German resistance to the euthanasia program is featured in most texts, apparently without recognizing the inconsistency of reporting the relative success of this resistance while contending that resistance to save the Jews would have been futile. Also, the fact that the top secret euthanasia program became widely known in Germany is not seen as a challenge to the view that the German people learned nothing during the war of the similarly secret Holocaust operations. It is often stressed in this connection, however, that the Holocaust killing factories were outside German Reich borders.

As mentioned above, textbooks portray the German people as having been largely ignorant of the genocide operations until the end of the war; however, a few recent texts have begun to challenge older ones. These assert that details of the *SS Einsatzgruppen* operations and mass gassings were known by a larger number of people than previously held. These books also discuss what is actually meant "to know" the extent and barbarity of the Holocaust during the war.

A common weakness of textbooks is the absence of conclusions about the meaning of the Holocaust or its accompanying events. It is not uncommon for German historical writing—especially on the subject of the Holocaust—to present the relevant factual data, but to pass over any inferences which may be drawn from them. The absence of conclusions, so apparent to the non-German reader, does not seem to have been noted by German observers who are perhaps more aware of the progress made over decades to get the factual elements of the subject into the textbooks. Less attention has been directed toward meanings and inferences than to factual narrative. In this regard, other countries, particularly the United States, have forged ahead in interpreting the meaning of the Holocaust in works of history, political science, philosophy, psychology, sociology and theology. German scholarship in general, it may be said, has been cautious and reserved in drawing major conclusions about this event. It has been especially difficult for German scholars to formulate conclusions which condemn the social, mental, or political attitudes of Germans of the Third Reich when these cultural patterns persist. The characteristics of love of order, obedience to authority, unquestioned fulfillment of duty, hierarchic organization, authoritarian personality structures and xenophobic social tendencies continue to exist in German society.

The function of textbooks in Germany—as in most countries—is generally the socialization of the nation's youth into the mainstream of contemporary society rather than the attempt to reform or revolutionize the basic mental attitudes of the society, a goal which possibly could lead young people out of the traditional socioeconomic and political framework of the nation. Thus, while a few innovative textbook authors may cite German scholarly works criticizing the authoritarian personality, the bureaucratic mind, and the economic practices of capitalism, these analyses are not integrated into a discussion of the Holocaust. Provocative textbook interpretations risk public censure and pressure on state authorities to ban their use. Textbooks for educating the young in history and politics are viewed as having the purpose of socializing young people to be self-respecting, loyal and proud members of the national community. To facilitate this, the search for a "usable past" continues. Should a large block of materials be seen as unserviceable for this purpose—as with the Holocaust—it will be dutifully reported so long as this is required, but the material will be left as an "erratic bloc,"—undigested, shocking, and only superficially assimilated, as a warning against dictatorship and a support for democratic government.

There are signs in the 1980s that West German scholarship may be on the threshold of coming to grips with many of the repressions of the past in confronting the Nazi legacy. There is a renaissance of Third Reich and Holocaust research in Germany which complements the worldwide explosion of Holocaust and related research which began in the 1970s. As a new generation of German scholars comes of age, increasing numbers of researchers have sufficient distance to examine the generation of their grandparents. Since the nationwide broadcast in West Germany of the U.S. NBC television series "Holocaust" in 1979, there has been a phenomenal growth in the number of books, articles, films, television programs, conferences, commemorations, university courses and local history projects, all of which signal an interest of a different kind than the "Hitler Wave" of the early 1970s. Along with a natural curiosity, that "Hilter Wave" included a great deal of nostalgia and admiration of Nazism. The new interest is more firmly determined to ask difficult questions about Germans, Nazis, Jews and genocide without the inhibitions and rationalizations which characterized earlier generations.   Moreover, the disquieting re-emergence of neo-Nazism and neo-racism in some citizens' attitudes toward Turkish workers living in Germany has given added import to what is taught about the Nazi past, about racial bigotry, and pluralistic values in the German school.

Chapter XIV

EVANGELICALS AND JEWS FORTY YEARS AFTER AUSCHWITZ

David A. Rausch

One month ago, on February 6, 1985, approximately one thousand evangelicals and Jews gathered in the Regency Room of the Shoreham Hotel in Washington, D. C. for the fourth National Prayer Breakfast for Israel. On the dais was a large spectrum of Jewish and Evangelical Protestant leaders from around the United States, including rabbis (from Orthodox to Reform) and clergymen (from Southern Baptist to United Methodist), academicians and businessmen, politicians and broadcasters. Those seated at the tables below represented an even broader spectrum. Before Israel's ambassador to the United Nations, Benjamin Netanyahu, addressed the eager participants, he was presented with a "Proclamation of Blessing" from the Evangelicals which read in part:

> We, representatives of Bible-believing Christianity, gather forty years after the Holocaust to affirm the importance of the State of Israel, and to unite with the Jewish people against those who wickedly assail them and their beloved State.

The relatives of those who died at the hands of the Nazis are threatened today by evil forces that would complete in word and deed the ghastly debacle that Hitler attempted.

A later passage continued:

> We hereby shed the Christian complacency so evident during the Holocaust and combat the anti-biblical, anti-humanitarian attitudes of those who would declare

"Zionism is racism," label terrorists as "moderates," and
deny the Jewish community their very peoplehood.

Both communities heartily applauded the presentation.

Nearby, at the National Religious Broadcasters Convention attended
by many of the Evangelical leaders, antisemites passed out anti-Israel
brochures and tracts filled with anti-Jewish code words and illustrations in
an effort to win some evangelicals to their racist cause. The two scenes
were indeed indicative of the heights to which Evangelical understanding
and commitment could soar and the pitfalls that face the movement at
every turn.

The contrast should not be ignored by the historian of the Holocaust
or of the Evangelical movement.   Some Evangelicals were on the
forefront of recognizing Adolf Hitler for what he was at an early date.
Others, such as Toronto clergyman and missionary statesman, Oswald J.
Smith, a decent man, were so blinded by their anti-Communism and by
the propaganda being disseminated by Christians in Germany, that they
felt in 1936 that Germany was in the midst of a religious revival. Why?
Because "born again" Christians in Germany told them so when they attended the Olympic Games.

American antisemites of that period, such as Gerald Winrod,
bolstered such a view and seared many a conscience by using biblical terminology to try to ensnare Evangelical Christians in a web of antisemitism. Both Hitler and Winrod were soon exposed, and the Evangelical movement was quick to accept the sordid reality that six million Jews
had been exterminated. Our friend, who is with us today, Dr. Carl Her-
mann Voss, who is *not* an Evangelical, can tell you of evangelicals who
were pierced to the core by the Holocaust and worked with him to al-
leviate the plight of the refugees while he headed the American Christian
Palestine Committee. Dr. Daniel Poling, Philadelphia editor of the *Christian Herald*, and Dr. John Bradbury, editor of the Baptist *Watchman-Ex-
aminer*, are good examples of such Evangelicals who worked with Dr. Voss.

Evangelical clergyman and educator, Dr. G. Douglas Young, was also
deeply moved by the Holocaust. While in the Ph. D. program at Dropsie
College for Hebrew and Cognate Learning at the end of World War II, he
was horrified at the graphic accounts circulated throughout the institution
on a daily basis. It disturbed him greatly that he, as a pastor in Nova
Scotia during the war, had entirely "missed" the reports of Jewish persecution until after the war and that Christians in general were silent. It was a
blow from which he never really recovered. He was determined that he
would never be silent again. For example, in the midst of Palestinian ter-
rorism in 1974, he defended the Jewish people, reminding Christians of
the Holocaust and concluded a letter to the *Jerusalem Post* ("Murdering of
Jews," May 17, 1974) by stating:

The moral bankruptcy of organized Christendom was
shown in the times of the Nazi holocaust when it failed to
speak out with one voice. Its moral fiber was tried and
found wanting. If it has really repented of that grievous
sin, it has an opportunity to prove it today by standing with
solidarity against these new genocidal movements.

Young's efforts at bridging the gap between the Christian and Jewish
communities are well known. In 1958 he founded the Institute of Holy
Land Studies in Jerusalem, a place where Evangelical students and faculty
could learn more about Israel, and in 1963 he and his wife moved to Israel. Until his death by heart attack in May of 1980, he was actively involved in the everyday pulse of the Jerusalem community. The people of
Jerusalem reciprocated his love by awarding him the Israel Pilgrim Medal
and, later, the city's highest honor, the "Worthy of Jerusalem" honor. At
his death, this evangelical statesman was given a crowning tribute by the
citizens of Israel which few Christians have attained—he was buried on
the crest of Mount Zion.

It is little wonder that at the *first* national conference between evangelicals and Jews, Dr. G. Douglas Young served as co-chairman with
Rabbi Marc H. Tanenbaum of the American Jewish Committee. And,
lest anyone view Evangelical and Jewish relationships as tenuous, let me
remind you that the progress has been phenomenal when one considers
that this serious dialogue took place only a decade ago, in December of
1975.

Since that time, two other national conferences have been conducted
and a number of regional conferences. More importantly, genuine interaction between Evangelicals and Jews is occurring on the level that G.
Douglas Young considered the most significant—the lay level, at the grass
roots.

With regard to the Holocaust and its remembrance, a number of interesting events have occurred since that first conference. Let me mention just a few. In a "Salute to America Bicentennial Congress on
Prophecy" held here in Philadelphia (July 3, 1976), Evangelical leaders
signed a document that stated in part: "The Holocaust, a racist act, is part
of Israel's sacred history, and although detractors of the nation claim this
to be a break in the covenant of God with the Jewish people....We believe
that the perpetrators of the Holocaust were in essence the enemies of
God, working against God and the eternal message of Israel...." Circulated
at rallies across the United States, thousands of other signatures were obtained in support.

In Chicago, when Nazi leader Frank Collin threatened to march in
predominantly Jewish Skokie, Illinois, sporting Nazi regalia that would
strike fear in the many survivors of the Holocaust who lived there, both

Moody Monthly (a family magazine) and its parent organization, Moody Bible Institute, took a firm stand to oppose such intimidation and terrorization. The Evangelical periodical declared that the march was contrary to human decency, immoral, contrary to Christianity and contrary to the spirit of American liberty.

Dr. George Sweeting, President of Moody Bible Institute, wrote the proclamation, "Our Pledge to the People of Skokie," where he stated in part, "We pledge to stand with the Jewish community. We want our friends to know that we oppose any propaganda and activity which makes Jewish people objects of hatred. We are committed to the pluralistic American society which honors every ethnic group." He concluded, "We urge Christian leaders and laymen to express their opposition to any action that would harm the American Jewish community."

On the West Coast, Evangelical groups have been opposing antisemitic outbreaks and groups that foster hatred. Evangelical publishers are beginning to sense the import of addressing such issues. A book on the history of antisemitism was published in 1981 by a popular evangelical publisher, Baker Book House. Baker has also published the proceedings of the first national conferences between evangelicals and Jews. Recently, another Evangelical publisher, Word Books, published Rabbi Yechiel Eckstein's *What Christians Should Know About Jews and Judaism* (1984).

Rabbi Eckstein, an Orthodox rabbi based in Chicago, has been involved in dialogue with Evangelicals for a number of years. Formerly with the Interreligious Affairs department of the Anti-Defamation League, he is founder and president of the Holyland Fellowship of Christians and Jews, an organization dedicated to promoting dialogue, reconciliation and better understanding between Christians and Jews. evangelical leaders have recommended his book, invited him to write articles for several Evangelical magazines, and asked him to speak in their churches, colleges and seminaries.

On the Reform end of the spectrum, Rabbi Joshua Haberman of the Washington Hebrew Congregation, has been a key supporter of Evangelical-Jewish dialogue and was even invited to write an article which appeared in *Action*, the voice of the National Association of Evangelicals. In the Evangelical Black community, Rev. Charles Mims, Jr., pastor of the Tabernacle of Faith Baptist Church in the Watts District of Los Angeles, has been a great supporter of the Jewish community and of brotherhood and dialogue. His deep love traces back to his childhood in the South where a Jewish storekeeper befriended him and his poverty-stricken family, and treated him as a beloved son.

These are only a few of the many individuals from the Jewish and Evangelical communities who have developed deep friendships. They are devoted to building bridges of understanding and dedicated to demolishing stereotypes and caricatures that have existed far too long. I, personally, have been impressed with the influence that the study of the Holocaust has had on such a process at both the leadership and lay levels.

And yet, I must confess with all candor that only the surface has been scratched. Like most Christians today, in spite of all the publicity and availability of materials, most Evangelicals know little about the Holocaust. In the early evangelical-Jewish dialogues, Holocaust history and its lessons has been one of the weakest areas. This is tragic, for today Evangelicalism is being bombarded with antisemitic materials and materials fostering religious and racial prejudice in an unprecedented fashion by a wide array of alluring groups that call themselves "Christian." Most of these groups demean the study of the Holocaust or deny that the Holocaust occurred.

I have taught courses on the Holocaust at a state university, on liberal arts campuses, and now on the graduate level. I have seen the profound changes that have taken place in students of all ages and from all walks of life. I have noted the changes in my own life as well. How sad, I feel, that a course on the Holocaust is not taught in most Christian colleges and seminaries, including both liberal and Evangelical institutions. Holocaust study enhances not only relationships with the Jewish community, but also an appreciation for all life, for all people of different ethnic, religious or racial backgrounds. It teaches one about structures of evil, the dangers of civil religion, and moral responsibility in an immoral environment.

Those of you from the East Coast are familiar with Evangelical theologian Dr. Marvin Wilson of Gordon College, and the encouraging results he has obtained by teaching the Holocaust as part of his Judaica courses. You know how active he has been in promoting the national conferences as well as the local initiatives. He is a true friend. Evangelical historian, Dr. Richard Pierard, who teaches a Holocaust course at Indiana State University, has also been deeply affected by the study. He wrote about his visit to Auschwitz in *The Covenant Quarterly* (February, 1975): "Try as I may, it was impossible for me to suppress the feeling that, if nothing more than because of sins of omission, I and my fellow evangelicals must share in the guilt for this incredible tragedy. With tears in my eyes I could only cry out in my inner being, 'Lord, have mercy on me and my brethren.'" There are others, but relatively few within the broad sea of Evangelicalism.

I felt that there was a need to have a text circulated by a respected Evangelical publisher on the many facets of the history of the Holocaust that would use this history as a case study of the racial and religious prejudice that is rampant today. I wanted this book to be reasonably priced, useful as a thought stimulator for survey courses in many areas (as well as a Holocaust course text), and yet readable enough for the average lay person. In July, 1984, this dream was realized when the book, *A Legacy of Hatred: Why Christians Must Not Forget The Holocaust*, rolled off the presses. I mention this only because of two reasons. The first is that the editorial board of the Evangelical publisher, Moody Press, envisioned the importance of this project—a project significantly different from any other book they have ever published. They plunged into the project with missionary fervor—a mission to Christians. They cared.

The second reason is the hundreds of letters I have received in response to the book from individuals who are hurting—who are battling the torturous tentacles of antisemitism. One woman from a northwestern state wrote recently that her father-in-law, who had initially been against the Internal Revenue Service, began subscribing to the *Spotlight* newspaper (published in Washington, D. C.) because it was also against the I. R. S. Most of us here are well acquainted with Liberty Lobby and the Carto network that publishes *Spotlight*, a network that has ensnared people of all walks of life. Now her father-in-law passes her and her husband horrid literature against the Jewish people. She sent me some that she noted was "not the worst"—it contained the blood libel and the infamous "quotes from the Talmud" to show how much Jews hate Christians. She knows nothing about Jews and Judaism, much less the Talmud. She only senses that something is wrong. She picked up my book in her church library and she needs help. Her letter informed me that she, her husband and her father-in-law are all "born again" Christians. When I checked on the population figures for her state, I found that there only 750 Jews in a population of 750,000. The synagogue nearest to her is over one hundred miles away (and she lives in the capital city!).

The letters come from those of all ages, all areas of the United States, all walks of life. There are great needs in this complex Evangelical Protestant community, a community where differences may be as great as those that separate Reform, Conservative and Orthodox Judaism. And I have found, dear friends, that these needs exist in the same proportion in the other Christian communities as well, regardless of a more Liberal theology or a higher social status. Antisemitism, in fact, infests the cultured parlors of our society, hiding behind a polished veneer of proper clichés and impeccable etiquettes. *Polite* racism is perhaps the most deadly racism.

It is a sad reality that evangelical magazines and journals give relatively little information to pastors and laypersons to combat misconceptions about Jews and to meet the educational demands of a proper Christian-Jewish relationship. Sunday School materials for children and young people have made a concentrated effort to eradicate any semblance of the "Christ-killer" theme (at least in the Evangelical community), cultivating instead a high regard for the heroes and heroines of the Jewish faith. Nevertheless, some adult study packets do insert this diabolical teaching, and teachers bring their own prejudice to class. Guidance is needed in regard to the dangers involved in fostering negative images of Jews and Judaism in the Sunday School curriculum.

It is ironic that Evangelical publishers of Sunday School literature have provided teaching guides of nearly every conceivable kind to facilitate their teachers in accurately portraying the topics of the Bible and to improve teaching techniques.   And yet, positive pointers on engendering proper views toward Jews and eliminating stereotypes (including the "Christ-killer" theme) from one's classroom are totally neglected. Because the same Scriptures and proof-texts are used yearly that have suffered misinterpretation for centuries, uninformed teachers from the elementary to the adult Sunday School level contribute to the propagation of negative images of Jews and Judaism (often unintentionally).   While this is also a very real problem for Liberal Protestants as well, evangelicals who use both the Bible and the Sunday School to a greater extent should be on the forefront of remedying such a situation.

The 1980s has also witnessed the steady growth of political right fringe movements that have sought to capture the heart and soul of Evangelicalism.   Their agenda and the implications of that agenda can no longer be ignored by the conscientious Christian.   Seemingly ethical leaders and theologians of the fledgling Christian Reconstructionist movement, for example, seek to create a society under the direct authority of "God's Law."   Taking their cue from Calvin's Geneva or the Puritan experiment in the Massachusetts Bay Colony, these men increasingly speak in naive terms of "Protestant nations" and "Christian nations" versus "pagan nations."   They are trying to convince a wary Evangelical movement that what the "decadent" United States needs is more *Christian* law practiced by more *Christian* lawyers, to bring in a *Christian* society with *Christian* economics to reach the world and make it *Christian*.   Castigated by a broad range of theologians and unable to convince Jerry Falwell of their "Christian nation" concept, they have, nevertheless, made inroads into a few Pentecostal and Charismatic Evangelical enclaves.   Especially susceptive have been the authoritarian "Shepherding" circles from the 1960s Jesus Movement.   Some ultra-Calvinist groups have also been drawn into their fold.   Intent on becoming a factor in Republican politics, lobbying efforts have been initiated, including an attempt to sway Pat Robertson and his Christian Broadcasting Network.

The obvious outsiders in such a system are the Jewish people.   And while the efforts of the Christian Reconstructionist Movement may well boomerang against them *and* the more moderate Evangelical community, they have taught us that even some Evangelicals are susceptible to the lure of the "Christian State" — a lure that has grave consequences for both Jews and Christians.   Christians must be taught that when one person's religious freedom is violated, all religious freedom is on the chopping block.   The Bavarian churches also thought they had a head start on a Christian society when a new government, one that claimed to foster "God's Laws" and to oppose "godless socialism," came into being.   Unfortunately the year was 1933, and the new regime was Adolf Hitler and his Nazi party.

Most of the leaders of the Christian Reconstructionist movement are naive "New Puritans," quite unaware of the ramifications of their perversions of the Bible and the tragedy of their politics. In contrast, racist "Identity" movements, with their British Israelite theology, openly and knowingly propagate antisemitism. Claiming that the white Anglo-Saxon Western peoples are destined to rebuild God's Kingdom and asserting that other "races" (including the Jewish people) are demonic or sub-human, the Identity propagandists are a threat to our entire body politic — including Evangelicals. Conspiracy theory and a survivalist mentality are their propaganda ploys to deceive a few Evangelicals. In addition, anti-Israel literature that was foreign to the fundamentalist-evangelical community in past decades is currently being spread in their churches at an alarming rate by men and women posing as "good Evangelicals" who "only want to clear up some false conceptions."

As in so many societies of the past, parents hold the key and children hold the future. I believe many parents today are hanging millstones of religious and racial bigotry around the necks of their children. Prejudice has no age of accountability. Young and old are subject to the venting of irrational hatred. History teaches us that the Nazis spent the largest portion of their time indoctrinating the young. A perusal of today's racist organizations would indicate the same policy. Children mimic the prejudices and values of adults. Keenly perceptive, they notice the judgments and damaging perceptions that we believe are safely hidden from them. Sometimes without realizing it, adults place "attitudinal stumbling blocks" in the path of a child's growth to maturity.

When a family attends a church, I believe an awesome responsibility is placed on the shoulders of the pastor and, in turn, the Sunday School teacher and youth leader. In some ways, they are a vital link between the family and their perceptions of other religions and races. With regard to Christian-Jewish relationships, the influence is much stronger because Christianity is so deeply rooted in Judaism and because Jesus was a Jew. Since there has been an historic antagonism between the two communities, the pastor who is not sensitive to the attitudes that he instills through the wording of his sermons and the reading of Scripture can build great barriers between his parishioners and the Jewish community.

I have already pointed out the importance of knowing the background to and the history of the Holocaust in the spiritual formation of a sensitive minister. This information must be passed on to the congregants. In addition, it is imperative for such a pastor to promote a respectful fellowship between his congregants and the nearest Jewish community. I believe that only when the two groups get together and nurture friendship are caricatures, stereotypes and distorted views then dispelled. Unfortunately, most seminary education today is a dismal failure when it comes to teaching a future pastor these traits.

In conclusion, as a historian, I believe that Evangelical-Jewish relationships are at a crossroads today. There is much potential for achievement, and plenty of room for wrong turns. In my estimation, Holocaust education is a significant key, and I firmly believe that the evangelical movement must not be written off by the Jewish community as unwieldy or impossible.   Misunderstandings and disagreements will occur and must be handled forthrightly and with patience.   Forty years after Auschwitz, relationships between Evangelicals and Jews are stronger than at any other time in history.

Chapter XV

ON THE CROSSROADS OF HOLOCAUST STUDIES FORTY YEARS LATER

Yaffa Eliach

Forty years ago, "the gates of Hell were opened," to quote the late Colonel Philans, the liberator of Dachau. Since then our minds, our hearts, our imagination, our faith, our dreams, and our nightmares, have been constantly preoccupied with the legacies of the dark kingdom. We are the generation burdened with the responsibility to make sure that the Holocaust will be remembered, that the world that was will be remembered by the world that is and the world that will be. We are that faithful bridge upon which a civilization rests. Whatever we record, restore, or transmit will become public record. Whatever we decide to ignore, to discard, or to overlook will disappear.

The unique vantage point is not our wisdom, it is a simple, biological factor, our age. We were there—we were there as executioners, we were there as bystanders, and we were there as victims. And we are still here today, fewer, but still, a very impressive group. There is no question that in our attempts to come to terms with the Holocaust we bring our personal biases. It is difficult to check them outdoors—we take them with us, no matter what we do, where we go. One traveling through Eastern Europe sees these biases not on a personal scale, but on that landscape of death where government made it a policy. One soon realizes that the Jews died a double death. First, they were physically killed; now their memory is being systematically erased and obliterated. Even in Auschwitz, which as a recent visitor liked to refer to as the "Disney World of death," the Jews were given one block. They exist there mainly in our own tormented minds and latent memories. The same is true for Babi Yar, for Ponar, for hundreds and thousands of graveyards in Europe. The Jews are not mentioned as victims who were killed there because they were Jews.

It is we, here, in this United States, and other places in the free world, who are in that unique position to make sure that the Holocaust will be recorded with accuracy. We here in other democracies, in the State of Israel, must take the lead in making sure that the Holocaust will be remembered, studied, and understood for what it was and for what should never, never, be allowed to be again.

There is no question today that we in America are leading in Holocaust-related activities. It is the sheer size of this vast country. It is the style of this country. I don't refer only to the mushrooming centers of Holocaust studies, that started first on the East Coast, but I refer to the ingenuity and the talent of hundreds and thousands of people involved in Holocaust studies across this United States. It was in America first.

It is right here somehow that interest in the Holocaust assumed a significant dimension. It was, at the very beginning, a grassroots movement. It started with the very young. I even remember at one point a very young author and journalist with a black turtleneck, by the name of Elie Wiesel, who was a lonely spokesman for the refugee community. Those were the days when refugees were known as "refugees," before the era of respectability when the name was changed to "Holocaust survivors." There were other names, too, but I'll only use the term refugees.

Slowly, it made its way from the street to the community to the synagogue, to the church, to the halls of universities, and only most recently it was adopted by the establishment. In Israel one may suggest that the process was in reverse: it was started by the government. First, there was a Yad Vashem and other institutions: Lohamei Hagettaot, Massuah, Yad Mordecai, and others. Then there was the Eichmann trial. Then there was the curricula in the schools. And only recently was there an involvement by a segment of the population, and the majority of them the Ashkenazi population. These two factors, that in America it started as a grassroots movement, and in Israel it started as a government movement, have great implications on the dimensions of Holocaust studies both here and in Israel.

The pluralistic nature of American society left its distinct mark on Holocaust studies and all other related Holocaust experience. It attracted outstanding individuals unmatched by any other field of studies in the United States. It also represents a cross section of American ethnic groups and American culture. They are outstanding academicians, people from the media, from universities, civic leaders, politicians, clergymen, and people from the West, the East, the North, the South and, of course, the Midwest too. They bring with them a dazzling array of talent that one cannot find in any other field. It makes Holocaust studies an interdisciplinary, exciting area, but at the same time each of these outstanding individuals, groups, and ethnic groups also bring to Holocaust studies their unique worldview, their unique ideology, and a unique point of view whch they at times do not pedal softly.

One can say that this is the greatest of Holocaust studies in the United States. However, at the same time, in this pluralistic culture, at times, when it comes to Holocaust studies, they do not have that center, they do not have the guidance. One important group among the many, many groups interested in Holocaust studies, are the survivors themselves. I am not sure that I share my views with them at all times, although I was introduced as a Holocaust survivor. At times, I think that our gatherings resemble class reunions. The Class of Auschwitz, 1935-45. I can sympathize with the social need of coming together and saying, "Here we are alive." But Holocaust survivors are the most precious commodity we have. They are the eyewitnesses and there are areas in Holocaust studies, that will remain grey areas if we do not interview them, for we do not have documentation. One cannot expect to find this kind of documentation in the official German archives.

Yet the many, many oral history projects that we have across the United States, in Israel, and in other places, as yet have not developed a system of not only how to interview, but also, a system of how to authenticate and verify the interviews they have done. We do not have the luxury of time to wait five or ten years. We must do it right now, for otherwise we will be missing perhaps the most essential aspect of the Holocaust, the humanistic aspect of it, for the spirit of human greatness can be found in the testimony of Holocaust survivors. But it cannot remain there as stories, it cannot remain there as testimonies because we know that the leading historians of Holocaust studies shun the testimonies of Holocaust survivors. I think it is something which must become first priority to centers of Holocaust studies across the United States, to undertake not only the recording but the method of turning some of these very important testimonies into documents.

There is another group which is also becoming prominent in Holocaust studies, and quite visible; the second generation, the children of Holocaust survivors. I would suggest that their movement started in the classes in Brooklyn College. I remember in 1971 and 1972 when 99% of my students were children of Holocaust survivors, among them the founders of the first generation in New York and subsequently in other cities across the country. I remember what it meant to face an audience who came to the class not for knowledge of the Holocaust—they came for any other reason you can think of but studying about the Holocaust. They wanted to find out why their mother cried, why their father had nightmares, who are the children in the picture on the piano, and so on. There was another percent in my class, the other one percent: they were the children of the American liberators, and they too came to find out why Dad kept pictures in the trunk somewhere in the garage or in the attic and will not share them with them. I can understand that bond of comradeship, the need of the children of Holocaust survivors to identify themselves as the second generation. But I think at times that this exclusivity is leaving out a large segment of young Americans. The same goes for the State of Israel, who has a genuine interest in the Holocaust and feel they do not have the credentials to be as active as they should be. When the movie *Kaddish* was shown in New York (by the way, it started as a project in one of my Holocaust classes in Brooklyn College with Yossi Klein), people were handing out leaflets and in the best New York fashion I just asked for one. It was a petition from the children of non-Holocaust survivors who also felt that they are excluded, that they would like to teach, they would like to study, they would like to share, they would like to be part of all the ongoing activities on the Holocaust, yet they felt they did not have the same "passport" (as one of them told me) to this unique society. I think we should rethink the place of the second generation and how it must open its heart, its doors to a much larger segment of those who are concerned and interested in Holocaust studies.

And, finally, there is another group: those of us who teach, study and write. Maybe we carry the heaviest burden of all, for what we say, what we write, what we remember and try to share with others, may become what will be remembered. It is almost fate to discuss curricula in this city, in Philadelphia; it is a good city for such a topic. Maybe because of your "French Connection." Maybe because one great Franklin follows another one. Maybe this is why you were able to create a curriculum in this city that can be envied even by us in the Big Apple. You are able to have one umbrella organization—it looks that way, I hope it's true—but indeed there is unity that other cities were not able to achieve. There are numerous curricula in the United States on the Holocaust. As a matter of fact, almost every city, county, state has its own curricula. Within every city there are a variety of curricula according to each shade and nuance in shade of opinion and political orientation. Indeed at times one feels that all who suffered come and join us in writing a curriculum. Everybody who suffered in this country and all over the globe is somehow included in American curricula on the Holocaust.

I am a buff of American Indian history. In none of the American Indian museums, or the books written about the American Indians, did I find any reference to the Holocaust, yet in almost every curricula that I pick up on the Holocaust there is a reference to the American Indians and many others. I think that we are mistaking the content of a curriculum with a methodology of making it relevant. Somehow there is a blurred distinction between the uniqueness of the event and its universal message, and how to bring across this universal message. As a matter of fact, we cannot be effective in our message and cannot analyze and diagnose any of the symptoms if the uniqueness of the event is blurred and lost in our teachings. I think it's time that we take that stand, although in a pluralistic society with the great American custom of equal time, each group is asking for equal time in a state or city curriculum. I recently saw one of them, a curriculum of a very great and large state, where the starving in the Ukraine was given equal time and space to that of the concentration camps. It is not unAmerican to bring to ones attention that in order to teach the Holocaust and bring its universal message we must preserve its authenticity. Only then can we be effective, in a country where discrimination existed, and where we have many ethnic groups. I think it is important to savor the privileges of each of the groups by identifying when there are symptoms of problems. By blurring the issues of the Holocaust the message will be lost.

I will never forget several among the many thousands of students who have come to the Center for Holocaust Studies, where we have a guide with a trained historian, and an exhibit, with a Holocaust survivor or a liberator assigned to the group. One a young black child said that after viewing our exhibits and after studying the segment on the Holocaust in her school that she had no sympathy for the Jews, neither did she have sympathy for Anne Frank, "for they are all pale-faced individuals who had the opportunity during the Holocaust to rip off the yellow star on the white arm band and mingle with the rest of the population," but she as a black child is not given that opportunity. No matter what she does, people will discriminate against her and identify her because she is black. Then somebody shouted from the same group, "You could always identify a Jew, even if he is pale-faced like everybody else, by his bulging pockets."

In another visiting group, the issue was brought up that according to the new family planning in China, it is estimated that about 20,000,000 little girls were murdered. A Jewish student shouted, "So what! They didn't care about us when we were murdered during the Holocaust. Why should I care about them?" And another young white student, when asked, "How would you feel if the Jews would disappear from your block, in your neighborhood?", responded "Quite good. The value of the property would go up."

I have cited three incidents; I can cite many more. These three youngsters were studying from a Holocaust curriculum that was prepared by their state or county. I became very interested in what kind of studies, what kind of guides they had, and since then I have become interested on a much larger scale because we constantly hear these kinds of remarks in places where Holocaust studies were introduced. It was interesting, that all of them were studying from a curriculum which was primarily based on primary documents, some of them illustrated, and the youngsters developed a greater affinity for the executioner there than for the victim. They identified with the Nazi regime with its order, with its efficiency, with its uniforms, with its flags, with its swastika, and could not identify with those miserable creatures in the striped uniforms. When I questioned the student who pointed out that you can always tell a Jew by his bulging pockets — as it happened he had a skiing cap in his pocket, and his pockets were bulging. He said to me that he saw this particular image in a cartoon from a German book that was distributed in Nazi schools and was now part of the curriculum he was studying. He remembered the image of hate, but did not remember his teacher's explanation why such cartoons would never, never appear in our press.

For the past years since these kinds of incidents — and they are mounting — one particular school in New York reports that incidents of antisemitism are up 16% since Holocaust studies were introduced. I am constantly preoccupied; what are we doing wrong in our curricula? Indeed, it is excellent that we are introducing Holocaust studies in the schools, but what kind of studies are we introducing? Maybe we are not too test-oriented and from somebody who is trained as a historian it may be the wrong statement to make — and my colleague Henry Friedlander will forgive me, for we share an office at Brooklyn College and debate the issue often. Indeed, should the sources be based on Nazi primary sources? Isn't this our responsibility to see that the curricula on the Holocaust be infused with a humanistic spirit? Maybe we are too document-oriented; perhaps it's time to introduce into our Holocaust studies a humanistic aspect. Maybe literature. Maybe when the child and the youngster will be able to identify not with the faceless individuals earmarked for destruction but will be able to identify with individuals; not the anonymous victims but people their own age, like themselves, with their fathers and mothers who lived in the country and one day were earmarked for destruction. Maybe our curricula should somehow create a balance between the facts, the documents, and the humanistic spirit. Seeing thousands of young people coming to the Center for Holocaust Studies, I see a real urgency if we are to continue to introduce the Holocaust in schools. It doesn't matter if it is public, if it is parochial. If it is ethnic, it does not matter because everybody has his own viewpoint, and it is much easier to identify with the oppressor in a society that sees so much violence than to try to identify with the victim.

In conclusion I would like to relate a Hasidic story: A Hasidic master once said, that when all lines of communication between men and men are broken, and between God and men are broken, maybe the only way to restore these lines of communication is to tell a story and to tell a tale. I think that maybe what the Hasidic master thought about was precisely our curricula. It is not enough to have the documents. To restore lines of communication, we must introduce a story, a humanistic element.

Some time ago a gentleman who was sick and knew that he was dying called his rabbi and told him, "Rabbi, I know that my days are numbered, and I would like very much when my time will come that I should be buried in my concentration camp uniform, the one in which I was liberated from Auschwitz." Indeed, a few days later he died. The rabbi said he could not deliver a eulogy since it was the holiday of Chanukah and on a holiday eulogies are not permitted. But he would like to share the following story, and he told them that Abe Bruckner from Forest Hills wanted to be buried in his concentration camp uniform. And when he asked him why, he said, "Listen, Rabbi, although I tried to be a good person, after all, who does not have transgressions? So when I appear before the heavenly court, I am afraid they will start to put all my transgressions on the heavenly scales of justice, and the scales will tip in my favor, for there is nothing more sacred, there is nothing more convincing, than a broken heart dressed in a concentration camp uniform."

Although I write Hasidic tales, I don't know what was the outcome in the heavenly court. This I am leaving for the Hasidic record. But I know that here on earth, at least for the next 40 years, we can make a difference in the scales of history and the scales of how the Holocaust will be perceived and what a young generation will learn about it. For whatever we put on that scale of justice, this is what will be remembered. Maybe, if we put the right curricula, if we give it much thought, maybe the black girl will understand that Anne Frank could not just rip off the yellow star because her neighbors would have betrayed her. Then the other girl will understand why you have responsibility if life is lost entirely, and then maybe that girl would wish that more people, more loving neighbors, would move into her neighborhood. Only then can we hope that indeed we are our brothers' and our sisters' keepers.

LIST OF CONTRIBUTORS

Yehuda Bauer is Professor of History in the Institute of Contemporary Jewry at the Hebrew University in Jerusalem. He is Editor of the journal *Holocaust and Genocide*, Director of the Vidal Sassoon Institute for the Scientific Study of Antisemitism, and author of several books on the Holocaust.

Jutta Bendremer is Assistant Professor of English at the Universtiy of Akron, Akron, Ohio. She is author of several articles on teaching the Holocaust.

Alan L. Berger is Chairman of the Jewish Studies Program and a member of the Religion faculty at Syracuse University, Syracuse, New York, His most recent book, *Methodology in the Academic Teaching of the Holocaust*, was published in 1988.

Harry James Cargas is Professor of Literature and Language, and Professor of Religion at Webster University, St. Louis, Missouri. The author of *A Christian Response to the Holocaust* and other works, he is Associate Editor of the journal *Holocaust and Genocide*.

Yaffa Eliach is Professor of History and Literature in the Department of Judaic Studies at Brooklyn College. She is also Director of the Center for Holocaust Studies and served on the U. S. Holocaust Commission under President Carter. She is author of *Hasidic Tales of the Holocaust*.

Wolfgang Gerlach is a regular columnist for the German weekly newspaper "Deutsches Allgemeines Sonntagsblatt." He has co-authored several theological anthologies on Church relations and served as a member of the Church of the Rhineland Synod.

Geoffrey H. Hartman is Professor of English and Comparative Literature at Yale University. He is a faculty advisor to the Yale Archive for Holocaust Testimonies.   He has published widely in the field of literary criticism and theory.

Jan Karski is Professor at Georgetown University School of Foreign Service. During World War II he served as a courier for the Polish underground carrying messages to leaders of the Axis powers. His *Story of a Secret State* is a classic.

Richard Libowitz is Rabbi of Congregation Ner Tamid, Springfield, Pennsylvania, Education Director of the Anne Frank Institute of Philadelphia and Lecturer in Theology at Saint Joseph's University. He edited *Faith and Freedom: A Tribute to Franklin H. Littell* and co-edited *Methodology in the Academic Teaching of the Holocaust.*

Franklin H. Littell is a Professor Emeritus in the Department of Religion at Temple University and Professor in the Institute of Contemporary Jewry at Hebrew University in Jerusalem. Often regarded as the "Father of Holocaust Education in America," he has authored numerous articles and books on the Holocaust. For the past 10 years he has written a weekly newspaper column, "Lest We Forget."

Marcia Sachs Littell is the International Director of the Anne Frank Institute of Philadelphia. She is the Director of the Annual Scholars' Conference and has edited *Holocaust Education: A Resource Book for Teachers and Professional Leaders* and *Liturgies On the Holocaust: An Interfaith Anthology.* She is a member of the Education Committee of the U. S. Holocaust Memorial Council.

F. Burton Nelson is Professor of Theology and Ethics at North Park Theological Seminary in Chicago, Illinois. He is an officer of the International Bonhoeffer Society, was Chairman of the 1986 Scholars' Conference on the Church Struggle and the Holocaust, and has published numerous articles in the field.

J. Williard O'Brien is Director of the Connelly Institute on Law and Morality, and Professor of Law at the Villanova Universtiy Law School, Villanova, Pennsylvania. He is an authority on professional ethics.

David A. Rausch is Professor of Church History and Judaic Studies at Ashland College, Ashland, Ohio. He has published many articles on Jewish/Christian relations, and his books include *Zionism Within Early American Fundamentalism, Messianic Judaism: Its History Theology and Polity* and *A Legacy of Hatred: Why Christians Must Not Forget The Holocaust.*

Walter Renn is Associate Professor of History at Wheeling College, Wheeling, West Virginia. He has published numerous articles on the status of Holocaust education in West Germany.

Evelyn Bodek Rosen is Professor of English at Community College of Philadelphia. She has worked extensively on community matters regarding Jewish/Christian relations and interracial understanding.

Robert W. Ross is Associate Professor at the Universtiy of Minnesota. He has published widely on the Holocaust and related issues including *So It Was True: The American Protestant Press and The Nazi Persecution of the Jews.*

Elie Wiesel received the Nobel Peace Prize in 1986. He is Andrew Mellon Professor in the Humanities at Boston University and has authored numerous books and articles on the Holocaust.

David S. Wyman is Professor of History at the University of Massachusetts at Amherst. His most recent book is *The Abandonment of the Jews: America and the Holocaust, 1942-1945.*

SYMPOSIUM SERIES